Ghost Stories of Ulster

**Featuring stories from the
paranormal investigating team
Ghost Searchers Ireland
and many of the
Game of Thrones locations**

Published by: Iveagh Publications

Editoral Team: Kieran Heenan
             Pauline McCrory
             Michael Wallace

Photographs by: Pauline McCrory

Book Designed by: M.A.W. Design
First Printed in N.Ireland October 2018, Reprinted October 2019.

ISBN 978-0-9927637-3-2

For other publications and projects check out our website:
www.annaclonehistory.com

Disclaimer

Although the authors and publishers have made every effort to
ensure that the information in this book was correct at press time,
the authors and publisher do not assume and hereby disclaim any
liability to any party for any loss, damage or disruption caused by
errors or omissions, whether such errors or omissions result from
negligence, accident or any other cause.

The authors are unable to verify the source of every photograph
used in this publication and apologise for any such photographs
that have been included without the permission of the owners.

Contents

Foreword   14 - 16

Chapter 1 - Haunted Castles   17 - 40

Glenarm Castle, Co. Antrim   17 - 18

Narrow Water Castle, Co. Down   18 - 19

Ballygally Castle, Co. Antrim   20 - 21

Burt Castle, Co. Donegal   21 - 22

The White Lady of Greencastle, Co. Down   22 - 24

Ross Castle, Co. Cavan   24 - 25

Northburg Castle, Greencastle, Inishowen, Co. Donegal   25 - 26

Dolly Munroe, the Ghost of Richhill Castle, Co. Armagh   26

Shane's Castle, Co. Antrim   27

The Ghost of Castlewellan Castle, Co. Down   27 - 28

The Ghost of Castle Chester, Co. Antrim   28 - 29

Killyleagh Castle, Co. Down   29 - 30

Nendrum Castle, Co. Down   30 - 31

Massareene Castle, Co. Antrim   31

Tully Castle, Co. Fermanagh   31 - 32

The Ghosts of Carrickfergus Castle, Co. Antrim   32 - 33

Castle Archdale, Co. Fermanagh   33

Crom Castle, Co. Fermanagh   33

Dunluce Castle, Co. Antrim   33 - 35

Castle Leslie, Co. Monaghan   35 - 36

The Ghosts of Doe Castle, Co. Donegal   36 - 37

Song – 'Maolmurra – a Ballad of Doe Castle'   38 - 39

Cabra Castle, Kingscourt, Co. Cavan   39 - 40

Chapter 2 - Ghost Searchers Ireland (G.S.I.)   41 - 56

Introduction   41 - 43

Personal Experiences of G.S.I. Members   43 - 50
- The Ghost Whisperer   44
- Charlie the Ventriloquist Doll   45
- The Man in Donaghadee   49 - 50

Some Places Visited by Ghost Searchers Ireland:-   50 - 56

Ram's Island Haunting, Lough Neagh   50 - 51

The Copeland Islands, Co. Down   51 - 52

The Ghost House, Newry   52 - 53

Donaghadee Town Hall, Co. Down   54

Carrickmacross Workhouse, Co. Monaghan 55

Benburb Priory, Co. Tyrone 55 - 56

Chapter 3 - Other Haunted Buildings 57 - 83

Crumlin Road Gaol, Belfast including G.S.I. Investigations 57 - 64

Armagh Gaol, Co. Armagh 64 - 65

The Raholp Funeral Ghost, Co. Down 65

Drumbeg Manor, Inver, Co. Donegal 66

Lissan House, Co. Tyrone 66 - 67

Ardglass Golf Club, Co. Down 67 - 68

Grace Neill's Public House, Co. Down 68 - 69

Dobbin's Inn Hotel, Carrickfergus, Co. Antrim 69 - 70

The Crown Bar, Belfast 70

The Abercorn Arms, Newtownstewart, Co. Tyrone 70 - 72

The Barracks, Ballyshannon, Co. Donegal 72 - 73

Haunted Police Station, Belfast 73

Sharon Rectory, Newtowncunningham, Co. Donegal 73 - 74

Springhill House, Moneymore, Co. Derry 74 - 75

Gillhall, Dromore, Co. Down 75 - 77

Flax House, Belfast — 77 - 78

The Ghosts of Pipe Lane Mill, Belfast — 78

Mussenden Temple, Co. Derry — 79

Molly the Friendly Ghost, Lisburn, Co. Antrim — 79 - 81

In Bed With a Ghost, Belfast and Loughinisland, Co. Down — 81 - 82

Ghost Forces Family to Emigrate, Rockacorry, Co. Monaghan — 83

Chapter 4 - Workhouse Ghosts — 83 - 90

The Blue Guardian, Glendermott Road, Waterside, Co. Derry — 84

Downpatrick Workhouse, Co. Down — 85 - 86

Tramps Terrified at Clones Workhouse, Co. Cavan — 86 - 87

Banbridge Workhouse, Co. Down — 87 - 88

The Union Workhouse, Lisburn Road, Belfast — 88

The Roe Valley Former Hospital, Limavady, Co. Derry — 89 - 90

Chapter 5 - Ghostly Tales of Churches & Other Places of Worship — 91 - 98

Bonamargy Abbey, Ballycastle, Co. Antrim — 91 - 92

Grey Abbey, Co. Down — 93 - 94

Drumballyroney Church Ghosts, Co. Down   94 - 96

Dunlewy Church, Co. Donegal   96 - 97

The Mystery of the Great Bell of Inch Abbey, Co. Down   97 - 98

Chapter 6 - Ghosts & Transport   99 - 117

York Road Old Railway Station, Belfast   100

Strabane Railway Station, Co. Tyrone   100

The South Armagh Ghost Train, Co. Armagh   101 - 103

The Railway Ghost of Ballymacarrett, Co. Down   103 - 104

The Ghost of Barnesmore Gap, Co. Donegal   104 - 105

The Phantom Car of Barnesmore Gap, Co. Donegal 105 - 106

The Girl from Ballymullan, Co. Down   106

Strange Happenings at Ballyjamesduff, Co. Cavan 107

The Roadside Ghost, Upper Lough Erne,   107 - 108
Co. Fermanagh

A1 Ghost Stories, Co. Down   108 - 109

Ghost Seen in Glencolmcille, Co. Donegal   109

The Snow Storm, Co. Cavan   109 - 110

Derry City Airport, Co. Derry   111

Warrenpoint's Ghost Ship, Co. Down   112

Ghostly Sightings on Carlingford Lough, Co. Down   112 - 116

The Ferryboat Ghost, Portaferry, Co. Down   116 - 117

Chapter 7 - Ghostly Tales about Animals   118 - 128

The Grey Man's Path, Ballycastle, Co. Antrim   118 - 119

The Hound of Iskaheen, Co. Donegal   119 - 120

The Headless Horse of Mullenakill, Co. Armagh   120

Haunted House in Moneymore, Co. Derry   120

The Black Dog of Morghen, Co. Antrim   121

Father Hegarty's Rock, Lough Swilly, Co. Donegal   121 - 123

The Wolfhound of Antrim Castle, Co. Antrim   123 - 124

The Stables of Tempo Manor, Co. Fermanagh   124

The Phantom Coach and Horses of Roskeen, Co. Tyrone   125

The White Horse Hotel, Co. Derry   125

Dundermot Mound, The Gateway to Hell, Ballymena, Co. Antrim   126

The Phantom Coach and Horses, Antrim Castle   126 - 127

The Galloping Coach, Portaferry. Co. Down   127

The White Gates, Ballymena, Co. Antrim   127

The Infamous Galloper Thompson, Belfast — 128

Chapter 8 - Haunted Places Throughout Ulster — 129 - 148

The Dark Hedges, Co. Antrim — 129 - 131

Rathlin Island, Co. Antrim — 131 - 133

The Piper's Cave, Ballintra, Co. Donegal — 134

The Blue Lady of Tollymore, Newcastle, Co. Down — 134 - 135

Bogey Hill, Newcastle, Co. Down — 135

Strange Sightings on Cavehill, Belfast — 135 - 136

The Ghosts of Drumbeg, Lisburn, Co. Antrim — 136 - 138

Mystery Man in Slievenaman, Mourne Mountains, Co. Down — 138

The Friar's Bush Graveyard, Belfast — 139

The Green Lady of Vicar's Hill, Co. Armagh — 139 - 140

The Old Railway Bridge, Sion's Mill, Co. Tyrone — 140 - 141

Ballyboley Forest, Larne, Co. Antrim — 141

Main Street, Ballymoney, Co. Antrim — 141 - 142

The Ghost of Emyvale, Co. Monaghan — 142 - 143

The Famous Finnis 'Ghost Tree', Dromara, Co. Down — 143

Biddy, the Ghost of Smithfield Market, Belfast — 143 - 144

Olivands Hill, Magherafelt, Co. Derry	144
The Castle Hole, Castlederg, Co. Tyrone	144 - 145
The Ballyroney Lake Ghost, Co. Down	145 - 146
The Lough Swilly Ghost, Co. Donegal	146
The Ghostly Boy, Giant's Causeway, Co. Antrim	147 - 148
Mystery Figure in Omagh, Co. Tyrone	148
Chapter 9 - Banshees & Other Death Warnings	149 - 165
Introduction	150 - 151
The Story of Finvola, Dungiven, Co. Derry	151 - 152
Ballad – 'The Gem of the Roe'	153
The Banshee of Newcastle Harbour, Co. Down	153
The Banshee of the Brandywell, Co. Derry	154
The Banshee of Shane's Castle, Co. Antrim	154 - 155
The Rathlin Island Banshee, Co. Antrim	155
Apparitions Before Death	155
The Mourne Doppelganger, Co. Down	156
Daylight Wraith in Cavankirk, Co. Tyrone	156 - 157
Boom Hall, Co. Derry	157 - 158

Floating Coffins in Attical, Co. Down — 158 - 159

Apparitions After Death — 159

The Sea Captain's Story, Bunbeg, Co. Donegal — 159 - 160

Vampires and Other Deathly Tales — 160 - 164

The Errigal Truagh Graveyard Story, Co. Monaghan — 160 - 161

Poem – 'The Churchyard Bride' — 162

Abhartach the Irish Vampire, Co. Derry — 163 - 164

Chapter 10 - Devil Related Stories — 165 - 179

Dr. Thomas Meredith's Sudden and Awful Visitation, Ardtrea, Co. Tyrone — 165 - 167

Cumber House, Claudy, Co. Derry — 167

The Tale of Stumpie's Brae, Co. Derry — 167 - 169

The Midnight Pact with Satan, East Co. Down — 170 - 172

Hell's Fire is Your Lot, Leitrim, Co. Down — 172 - 174

Galgorm Castle, Ballymena, Co. Antrim — 174 - 175

Hawkin's Ghost, Rathfriland, Co. Down — 175 - 177

The Devil and the Gamblers, Co. Derry — 177 - 178

A Dance with the Devil, Hilltown, Co. Down — 178 - 179

Chapter 11 - Poltergeist Stories   180 - 188

The Cooneen Poltergeist, Co. Fermanagh   180 - 182

The Drumfanad Ghost, Co. Donegal   182 - 183

The Trinity Street Ghost, Belfast   183 - 184

The Larne Poltergeist, Co. Antrim   184 - 185

The Derrygonnelly Farmhouse Ghost, Co. Fermanagh   185 - 186

Strange Happenings in Articlave, Co. Derry   186 - 187

Mysterious Happenings in Magilligan, Co. Derry   187

Mysterious Noises near Bridge End Railway Station, 187 - 188
Inishowen, Co. Donegal

Chapter 12 - Ancient Myths & Legends   189 - 197

The Last Serpent of Ireland, Lig na Paiste, Co. Derry   189 - 191

The Lough Shannagh Monster, Co. Down   191 - 192

Finn McCool Legends   192 - 194

The Ardboe Cow, Co. Tyrone   194 - 195

Saint Bronach's Well, Rostrevor, Co. Down   195 - 197

Ossian's Grave, Cushendall, Co. Antrim   197

Annaghmare Court Tomb, Co. Armagh   197

Chapter 13 - Other Mysteries & Unusual Stories   198 - 203

The Haunted Gates of Finnebrogue, Co. Down   198 - 199

Lurgan Woman Buried Twice, Co. Armagh   199 - 200

Belvoir Park Hospital, Belfast   200 - 201

The Mysterious Lady in Blue, Buncrana, Co. Donegal   201

Unsettled Corpse, Creeve, Pomeroy, Co. Tyrone   201 - 202

The Vanishing Village of Audley's Town, Co. Down   202 - 203

The Cracked Tombstone in Newtownbreda
Churchyard, Co. Down   203

Bibliography   204 - 206

Glossary   207

Foreword

"The Supernatural is the natural not yet understood"

Elbert Bubbard (1856-1915)

"The Supernatural is the natural not yet understood" Elbert Bubbard (1856-1915). Ireland is an ancient land and has a rich history of folklore, mythology and conflict and it is no surprise that there are so many ghost, banshee and fairy sightings all around the country and the Province of Ulster is no exception.

Ghosts may take the form of phantom white and blue ladies, ghostly nuns, children, animals and horse-drawn carriages. Other ghosts make their presence felt through unexplained lights or noises which occur in haunted houses. Ghostly happenings occur in castles, cottages or even open spaces.

Many years ago when there was no electricity, television or the Internet, such tales were kept alive by word of mouth. People would gather in their cottages and over a turf fire, tell stories and legends about Celtic heroes such as Cuchulain and mythological people such as the Tuatha De Danaan. In rural areas, stories were also told about ghostly sightings, fairies, leprechauns, witches and the dreaded banshee. Every part of Ireland has its own collection of individual tales and mysterious happenings. These stories were handed down over generations.

Ghost hunting has become popular in this part of Ireland and around Halloween there are a number of 'ghost tours and walks' arranged in some of our popular haunts, for example, Crumlin Road Gaol.

Recently, this part of Ireland has become the location for the filming of the hit HBO Series 'The Game of Thrones' and many of the locations have a ghostly past and are featured in this book. The recent 'Star Wars' movie was filmed in Inishowen in Co. Donegal-another area with an ancient and mythical past as described in the book.

This publication focuses on Ulster and its nine counties namely Antrim, Armagh, Cavan, Donegal, Down, Derry, Fermanagh, Monaghan and Tyrone. (See Glossary). Special reference has been given to filming locations of the HBO Series 'Game of Thrones' which has used many of the iconic parts of N. Ireland.

We have concentrated on stories about people who have experienced paranormal activity in one form or another allowing the reader to experience these personal accounts first hand. Other stories have been passed down over the years by word of mouth or have been unearthed during research of old books and newspapers.

Our publication covers haunted buildings and places including the many castles across Ulster. We also provide stories of the dreaded banshee, poltergeists and devil related tales from across the country. We journey back in time to retell the ancient mysteries and legends of Ulster including those of Finn McCool and the story of the Lough Shannagh monster in the Mourne Mountains of County Down. We are indebted to Ghost Searchers Ireland who have provided some of their paranormal experiences. Finally, we have included some of the strange and mysterious stories that we came across in our research.

Even though the tradition of storytelling in modern Ireland has dwindled, there is still a fascination with ghost and fairy stories and mysteries. We hope that this publication will re-generate further interest in the 'Other Ireland' and rekindle the tradition of storytelling. The authors would like to thank all those who contributed or assisted in any way with this publication.

As you read through the book, we would ask the reader, *"Are you a believer or a sceptic?"*

Whether you are a believer or not, remember that most of these stories originated from first-hand accounts and many of the people who told us the stories did not believe in ghosts either. However, as the saying goes, 'seeing is believing' so always remember to be on the lookout as you never know what might be lurking in the shadows. You might even feature in our next book!

Chapter 1
Haunted Castles

Ghost Stories from the Many Castles around Ulster

Nearly every old castle has a ghost story linked to it and those in Ulster are no exception.

Glenarm Castle, Co. Antrim

Situated on the Antrim Coast about forty miles from Belfast, there has been a castle here since 1242, which was built by the Norman, John Bisset. The castle has been in the McDonnell family for over four hundred years and many ghostly sightings have been reported over its long history.

In the 19th Century, the same female ghost was observed by many people walking near the guest bedrooms. She was described as tall and wearing an old fashioned dress and a frilly bonnet. A group of children were also observed playing in the gardens and when approached, they simply disappeared. Another sighting involved a ghostly male figure dressed in uniform that always seemed to be in a hurry but vanishes near the front porch.

The Barbican, Glenarm Castle

Another story was reported from Hector McDonnell who grew up in Glenarm Castle. He said that his mother was forced to have every room in the castle, except the attic, 'exorcised' as she was so fed up with all the paranormal activity. Hector used to hear heavy footsteps coming from the attic and one of the maids sent him into the attic to investigate. He turned on the attic lights from the base of a stairway but as soon as he entered the room, the attic light was turned off, even though he was on his own. Just before he managed to descend the stairs in the darkness, he felt that someone was behind him. He never entered the attic again!

The noises from the attic continued for many years and no one apart from himself would sleep in that part of the castle.

Narrow Water Castle, Co. Down

Narrow Water Castle lies on the shore of Carlingford Lough just outside Warrenpoint and is reputed to be haunted by a squire who was cursed by a local priest. Many years ago, the priest was given a brutal whipping by the squire. Afterwards the priest cursed him to choke to death as a punishment. It is claimed that the ghost of the squire can be heard crying out with a dreadful gurgling sound similar to that of a person who is indeed choking.

Another story relates to the ghosts of soldiers being seen on the road between Newry and Warrenpoint near Narrow Water Castle. In August 1979, eighteen soldiers were killed during a two-stage bomb planted by the IRA. The attack was carried out as a convoy of two army trucks made its way from an army base in Newry. Its route took it past the castle. An 800 Lb. bomb was hidden in a trailer at the side of the road concealed among bales of straw. It detonated as the rear convoy passed by. It is believed that six soldiers died in the first explosion. The remainder were killed by a second explosion as they took up a defence position behind nearby gates and a wall.

Since then, many motorists passing through that area, have claimed to have seen soldiers standing at the side of the road. Some drivers have even pulled into the hard shoulder thinking that it was an actual checkpoint. When they reach the side of the road there is no one there!

On another occasion a man pulled in and got out of his car to go to the toilet and when he looked around there was a soldier beside him. Needless to say he did not take the time to zip up his trousers before getting back into his car and hurrying away from the scene.

Narrow Water Castle near Warrenpoint, Co. Down

Ballygally Castle, Co. Antrim

Ballygall(e)y is situated about three miles north of Larne. Its name is derived from 'Baile Geithligh', which means the 'Townland of Geithleach'. Ballygally castle was built around 1615 and later extended to form a Georgian farmhouse; it is now a famous hotel.

Ballygally Castle, Co. Antrim

It is said that the ghosts have been haunting Ballygally Castle for over four hundred years. The most well known ghost is that of Lady Isobella Shaw, the wife of Lord James Shaw. One story states that she was unable to give birth to a son and therefore an heir to the estate. Her husband locked her inside one of the rooms at the top of the castle as punishment. During an attempt to escape, she fell to her death and her ghost is said to be still haunting the castle.

Despite her tragic story, she is said to be a friendly ghost and Ballygally Castle Hotel, has named one of its rooms in the tower after her. People who stayed below the 'Ghost Room' in the tower have heard unexplained noises and even the sound of children running and laughing even though no one was there. Lady

Isobella's ghost is said to knock on doors of the bedrooms and then disappear. Several visitors have stated that they felt her presence in the rooms.

Another ghost in the castle is that of Madame Nixon who used to live here during the 19th Century. She has a well named after her. Her ghost has been seen walking around the hotel and she is recognisable by the rustling of her long silk dress.

The hotel brochure actually mentions its ghost – 'the hotel is reputedly haunted by a friendly ghost, Lady Isabella, and brave guests can visit the *'ghost room'* in the Tower!'

Burt Castle, Co. Donegal

Burt is close to the town of Newtowncunningham in the Inishowen Peninsula. The name 'Burt' comes from the parish of 'Caisleán Bhirt'. Burt Castle was built on the shores of Lough Swilly during the reign of Henry VIII (1509-1547). One of the chieftains who lived there was Cahir O'Doherty who as a result of rebelling against the king lost the castle. Burt has been the site of many battles over its long history and some say that is why there is an air of menace that surrounds the castle.

Burt Castle, Co. Donegal

One story exists of how a young girl became pregnant to one of the kingsmen of O'Doherty. He refused to marry her and she became very distraught. As she walked the shores of Lough Swilly, it is said that a number of swans swam over to her and called her into its deep cold waters where she drowned. Her father swore revenge and tricked his way inside the castle and killed the man responsible for his daughter's misfortune. He threw the man's body from the castle. When the moon is full, it is said that swans have been seen congregating near the castle and start to wail and cry. Then the ghostly figure of a young girl is seen entering the water and then slowly disappearing beneath the waves. At the base of the castle there is a patch of grass that withers when the swans cry. It is said that this is the spot where the body of the man who wronged the young girl fell to his death.

The White Lady of Greencastle, Co. Down

During the 16th century, H. Rupert de Burgh was the Lord of Greencastle. On a trip to Rome, Italy, the young lord fell in love with a beautiful girl called Jeanne Pearlin. Although she at first rejected all his advances, she eventually agreed to marry him. The young couple was very happy at first but then de Burgh started to tire of his new fiancée. Rather than break off their engagement, he decided to take the cowardly decision to return home. He claimed that he had urgent family business to attend and needed to go home immediately.

The young Jeanne was dismayed and pleaded for him to take her with him. Just as his carriage was leaving, she opened its door and tried to enter. De Burgh pushed her back and demanded that the driver proceed as quickly as possible; Jeanne fell back and was run over by one of the wheels and was so badly injured that she died. De Burgh never looked back and fled back to Greencastle as quickly as possible.

It was quite late when he eventually arrived home and just as his carriage reached the gates to the castle, the horses stopped and refused to move any further.

De Burgh looked out to see what the delay was and was horrified by the sight of a white gleaming face peering down at him from the top of the stone archway, which stood over the entrance gates. A hand then reached upwards to the face and pointed to its forehead, which bore the marks of a ghastly wound. De Burgh looked closer and realised that this face was that of his dead fiancée Jeanne.

The horses then suddenly bolted forward and as the carriage entered through the gates, he could hear a loud mocking laugh. That night many strange things happened in the castle. Servants could hear doors opening and closing and the sound of tiny feet running along the stone corridors. These hauntings continued for a long time. De Burgh did marry again but he and his new wife died soon after and the castle passed into other hands.

Many years later, one of the maids who worked in the castle got engaged to a local man. One night they agreed to meet in the castle grounds after their work was done for the day. Her fiancé arrived first and waited for her but she was delayed and soon it got very late. Midnight arrived and he could see the figure of a young woman coming towards him. Thinking this was his fiancée; he ran to meet her and threw his arms around her. But he only clasped air. The figure appeared to run through him and continued on her journey through the garden. He could not understand what had happened and being curious, he followed. He could not catch up with her but after some time, the path split and it was only then that the figure turned around. It revealed a face that made him recoil in horror!

Her hand pointed up to a gaping wound in her forehead. The figure turned around again and continued on its journey.

As one can imagine, the young man was frozen to the spot but he did eventually manage to return home where he later told his story. This was indeed the ghost of the 'White Lady' once again haunting the old castle!

After de Burgh, the castle at Greencastle was passed to the Magennis's, then to Nicholas Bagnal and eventually to the Needham family. It is now in ruins but many other ghost stories are attached to this old castle. Centuries ago, a ship from a strange land was seen to dock at Greencastle Pier. A very small man came ashore alone and made his way to the castle. However, he was never seen leaving or in fact never seen again so no one knows of his fate.

After midnight following his arrival, everything in the castle went berserk. All the animals started roaring; pots and pans rattled and old clock fell from a wall to the ground. This commotion continued every night until the local clergy decided to carry out an exorcism. Whatever or whoever was causing the noise was ordered to be banished from the area for at least five hundred and twenty years. The spirit was not happy about this but the clergy stuck to their original demand. No one knows what will happen when the five hundred and twenty year period expires. Some say that this event will happen very soon.

Ross Castle, Co. Cavan

Ross Castle is located on the shores of Lough Sheelin south of Mountnugent in Co. Cavan. The castle was built by Richard Nugent in the mid 16th Century. Richard was also known as 'The Black Baron' as he had quite an evil reputation. His only daughter Sabina fell in love with Orwin who was the son of O'Reilly, an archenemy of the Black Baron.

The young couple could see no future for their relationship here so decided to elope. Unfortunately, Orwin was drowned in the lough and Sabina fell into a deep despair locking herself away in the tower of the castle. She would not eat or drink and died of a broken heart. Her ghost is said to haunt this part of the Castle, which is now a hotel. It is also claimed that her father, the Baron also haunts the Castle as he grieves for the loss of his only daughter.

Ghost Searchers Ireland visited the castle and concluded that it is a very spiritual place. The group split into several teams and all experienced strange phenomena including lights going off and on, door handles moving and noises and bangs. They also witnessed a dressing table mirror move of its own accord. Caron noticed the smell of lavender. When the team used the Franks Box, there were recorded answers to a number of questions and at one stage the team were told to "*get out*"!

Northburg Castle, Greencastle, Inishowen, Co. Donegal

Now in ruins, this castle was built in the 14th Century by the Norman, Richard de Burg. It stands on a promontory overlooking Lough Foyle.

Northburg Castle, Co. Donegal

The ghost story relates to the forbidden relationship of two young lovers, namely the daughter of Earl William and the son of Sir Walter Burk. Both of their parents were archenemies and when Earl William discovered the relationship, he locked the young man in a tower to starve to death. William's daughter would sneak in food and water to the prisoner but when she tried to rescue her lover, she was killed. The story goes that as a punishment for helping the prisoner, she was thrown from the battlements. The pair are now said to be reunited as ghosts and haunt the old castle, no longer in fear.

Later, the castle became a stronghold of the Clan O'Doherty and was damaged by canon fire. It fell into ruins shortly afterwards in the 17th Century.

Dolly Munroe, The Ghost of Richhill Castle, Co. Armagh

Richhill was originally known as Legacorry. Richhill Castle was built in the 17th Century by the Richardson family who had married into the Sacheverall family, the local landowners. Various families occupied it up to the present day but part of the castle has fallen into ruin and it is said to be home to several spirits.

The most famous one is Dolly Munroe who was married to William Richardson, the son of Major Edward Richardson an M. P. and High Sheriff of Armagh. The latter had married into the Richardson family. At the age of seventeen, Dolly was reputed to have been the most beautiful girl in the whole of Ireland. She died in 1793 and did not have any children. Many sightings have been seen and strange occurrences have taken place.

As a location it has been the subject of many paranormal investigations. One story is told of a visitor to the castle who chatted to the spirit of a lady on the stairs and reckons it was the ghost of Dolly.

Shane's Castle, Co. Antrim

Shane's Castle is located near Randalstown and was built in 1345 on the north eastern shore of Lough Neagh. Originally known as Eden-duff-carrick, it was reinstated to the O'Neill chieftains in 1607 by King James. From then on it was known as Shane's Castle after Shane O'Neill.

The estate stretches over 2,600 acres and it has provided a versatile location for many Game of Thrones scenes, one of which was the Tourney of the Hand in honour of Ned Stark. Also when King Robert Baratheon and posse came to Winterfell, and the King's Landing dungeons. The castle grounds have provided locations for the frozen northlands of Westeros and one of its arched bridges has been utilized in a number of scenes including the sword fight between Brienne of Tarth and the Kingslayer. The shores of Lough Neagh nearby were used when Brienne of Tarth dispatched a group of wild men escorting Jamie Lannister to King's Landing.

One of the Castle's tower walls contains an ancient stone carving of a head, known as the black head of the O'Neill's, or the black brow on the rock. It is said that the O'Neill line will end when the head ever falls off. Luckily, the head has survived even when the castle's banshee set fire to the castle (See Chapter 5). Several spirits are known to haunt the castle and its grounds. When a fire started in the old castle in 1816, it was evacuated, but a man in armour was seen passing by the upstairs windows.

The Ghost of Castlewellan Castle, Co. Down

This story originated from staff who used to work in the castle in the early 1900s. It was a dark winter's night when one of the servants heard a loud noise coming from one of the upstairs rooms. When he went to investigate, he saw a large figure dressed in white emerging very fast from one of the bedrooms. It seemed to the servant that the figure was trying to escape from something or someone and was very frightened. The servant was also frightened by what he had seen and ran to his own room where he locked himself in for the rest of the night.

Over the years, the same servant claimed to have seen the figure again coming out of different rooms at night. He was convinced that the spectre was one of the Annesley family who used to live in the castle. When he mentioned seeing the ghost to the then current Lord Annesley, he was laughed at. His master told the servant to go to bed earlier rather than creeping around the castle late at night.

Castlewellan Castle, Co. Down

The Ghost of Castle Chester, Co. Antrim

The ruins of this castle can still be seen in Whitehead and it dates from before the 12th or 13th Century. It gets its name from the Chichester family who lived there from the 16th Century.

Back in the 18th Century, a butler from the nearby Redhall Mansion fell in love with Beth, one of the maids of Castle Chester.

He was besotted with her but she did not feel the same way. One day, he begged her to marry him and when she refused, he took out a phial of poison and quickly drank it. He collapsed in agony and died at her feet.

After he was buried, some strange things started to take place around the Castle. Another maid saw the dead man standing beside the path as she fetched some water. Strange noises were heard throughout the night and the doors were repeatedly opened and banged shut. Everyone became very frightened and it was decided to carry out a thorough search of the building. As they went downstairs, all the candles were blown out the women screamed and one of them fainted.

After a number of nights of this activity, it was decided to bring in the local priest. He advised that the body of the butler should be reburied in the bed of a nearby stream and therefore lay his ghost to rest in peace. All was quiet for a few days until one of the servants was taking a horse and cart across the stream over the castle's driveway when the dead man reappeared. He jumped into the cart beside the servant and reached out a partly decomposed hand. The servant immediately collapsed and was found unconscious in the back of the cart. Meanwhile, the horse galloped up to the castle yard and was in a terrible state - foaming at the mouth, sweating and seemingly scared out of its wits.

It was not until the next morning that the servant was able to describe what had happened to him. The priest was summoned again and he asked that the body of the butler, be laid to rest for the third time in the sand on the nearby beach with boulders placed over the grave. After this, peace again returned to the castle.

Killyleagh Castle, Co. Down

Killyleagh is derived from 'Cill Ó Laoch' meaning 'the church of the descendants of Laoch'.

The castle itself dates back to the 12th Century when it was built by John de Courcy and has been owned by the Rowan-Hamiton family since the 17th Century and extended. During the Civil War, the owners were the Count and Countess of Clanbrassil. They supported the Stuart Monarchy but paid the price when Cromwellian Forces besieged the castle in 1649. The Countess Clanbrassil was a formidable lady and had rallied the villagers to create a stronghold. She negotiated a deal to save her family and her home and managed to get a pardon for her husband.

It is said that her ghost roams the castle to this day, as she loved it so much. The castle was also the birthplace of Hans Sloane the famous London physician and patron of the British Museum.

Killyleagh Castle, Co. Down

Nendrum Castle, Co. Down

Also known as Mahee Castle, it lies on Mahee Island in Strangford Lough and was erected by an English Soldier - Captain Thomas Browne in 1570. The castle lies close to Nendrum Monastery, which dates from the 5th Century. The abbot of the monastery,

Setna Ua Deman was burned to death in his home in the 10th
Century, most likely by Vikings. It was abandoned as a church
in the 15th Century. In 1922, H.C. Lawlor excavated it and it is
claimed that the removal of several holy items upset the many
spirits who exist in the castle. These spirits are mostly described as
monks.

Massereene Castle, Co. Antrim

This once grand castle, also known as Antrim Castle and was built
in the mid 17th Century on the banks of the Sixmilewater River.
It was demolished in the 1970s after suffering a fire and neglect.
All that remains is an Italian style tower built in 1887, the remains
of the original castle and a Gatehouse. Its formal gardens are very
popular to visitors having been restored by the local council.
Antrim Castle Gardens won the Ulster in Bloom Special Award in
2012.

Tower of Massereene / Antrim Castle

The ghost of a servant girl Ethel
Gilligan is said to walk the
castle gardens. Originally from
Westmeath, she was rescued
from a fire in the castle in 1922
but later died from smoke
inhalation. Locals refer to her as
'the white lady'.

Two other stories from this
castle are to be found in
Chapter 6 - Ghostly Tales about
Animals.

Tully Castle, Co. Fermanagh

The ruins of Tully Castle lie near Lough Erne. It dates from the
17th Century and was formally built and owned by Sir John Hume

as part of the Plantation of Ulster. During the 1641 Rebellion, the castle was attacked by Roderick Maguire in 1641 and everyone inside was killed.

The same ghostly figures have been seen over the centuries usually around Christmas when the massacre occurred, namely two figures leading with a horse at a fast trot around the castle's foundations.

The Ghosts of Carrickfergus Castle, Co. Antrim

This is a Norman Castle dating back to the 12th Century built by the de Courcy family and has a long and varied history. It was besieged by King John, captured by Edward Bruce and then William III in 1689. It has many stories of cruelty and deaths including one that claims that hundreds of captives were thrown over the walls of the castle into the sea by Cromwellian Forces in 1641.

Carrickfergus Castle, Co. Antrim

One ghost is that of a young soldier, Tim Lavery who met a very violent death, as he was found guilty of murder despite the fact that it was his friend who had committed the crime. It is claimed that Tim cursed his former friend and that he and others would have no rest for killing an innocent man. Tim was also known as 'Buttoncap' as he wore a large button in the centre of his cap. His ghost, who carries his head under his arms, walks the battlements of the castle.

Castle Archdale, Co. Fermanagh

This castle was built by the Archdale family during the Ulster Plantation. The early castle was destroyed by the Maguire Chieftains and it is said that all of the Archdale children were killed with the exception of one who was saved by a nurse who threw him out of a window. The screams of the children are often heard as well as the ghost of the nurse.

Crom Castle, Co. Fermanagh

Owned by the Earls of Erne, this castle is situated on a lakeside near Newtownbutler. It was built in the 17th Century and was set on fire in 1764. A mysterious ball of light has been seen rolling over the lake and witnessed by many of the locals and visitors alike. The light is supposed to be as a result of a curse or a spell.

In the grounds of Crom Castle lies a massive yew tree, apparently the largest in Ireland and able to shelter at least two hundred people. Locals claim that the tree can talk – voices have been heard coming from the tree over the centuries and no other source can be identified.

Dunluce Castle, Co. Antrim

The name Dunluce is derived from 'Dúnlios' meaning a fortress or fortified residence. The Castle itself lies in ruins today but was a strategic site overlooking the sea between Ballycastle and Portrush. It is thought to date from the 13th Century by the McQuillan chieftains and sits on top of a rocky outcrop 100 feet above the raging sea below. The Clan MacDonnell's then took the castle before it changed hands again. It has seen many tragedies over its long history and there are said to be many ghosts that haunt the ancient ruins.

Dunluce Castle, Co. Antrim

Richard Og McQuillan inherited the castle at an early age but he soon became a very powerful man and oppressed the local people in his estate. It is said that he was doomed to remain on earth because of his evil past.

McQuillan's daughter was called Maeve Roe. She was a strong willed girl and against her father's wishes she fell in love with one of the officers in his army called Reginald O'Cahan. Lord McQuillan did not approve of this match as he had other plans for his daughter's future.

He locked Maeve inside of the towers of the castle. Her lover, Reginald climbed the external wall of the tower and with Maeve on his back, managed to free her and descend once again. At the bottom, they climbed into a small boat and went out to sea. Unfortunately, a storm arose and they were tossed towards a rocky outcrop and they perished, crushed against the jagged rocks. It is said that on stormy nights, one can still hear Maeve wailing in the tower and out in the storm she can be seen searching for her long lost love.

There is another legend from 1639. One very stormy night the entire kitchen of the castle collapsed into the sea below and apparently eight workers lost their lives as they fell onto the rocks below. Their screams can still be heard to this very day and especially on stormy nights.

C.S. Lewis, the famous author, is reputed to have been inspired by the magnificent ruins of the castle for the Royal Castle of Cair Paravel in the Chronicles of Narnia. It has also been used as a location for the Game of Thrones series for the fire-scorched Castle of Harrenhal and the Castle at Pyke.

Castle Leslie, Co. Monaghan

Castle Leslie is a privately owned large estate in Glaslough, Co. Monaghan and now used as a successful hotel and equestrian centre. It was bought in 1655 by the Bishop of Clogher and then developed by the Leslie family, originally from Scotland. There are reports of several members of the family who haunt the large mansion.

Norman Leslie was seen in the Red Room by Lady Majorie Leslie some weeks after he had been killed during WWI. He appeared to be reading some letters and when she asked him why he was here, the ghostly figure just turned towards her and smiled before he vanished. It is also said that just before her death in 1951, Lady Margorie appeared at her son's London residence. One of her grandchildren was very ill and she was seen rushing into the baby's room and touching it before disappearing. The baby, Sean suddenly murmured *"pain gone"*. He had been cured!

Castle Leslie, Co. Monaghan

The Mauve Room is said to be haunted by Lady Constance Leslie. One story involved a lady named Leonie, a visitor to the castle, but who unfortunately was dying in the Mauve Room. Her nurse witnessed an elderly lady approach Leonie and speak to her before she suddenly vanished.

After the funeral, the family and the nurse were sitting in the dining room when the nurse noticed one of the family portraits; she became very concerned, as it was the same lady who had visited her dying patient days before! It was Lady Constance!

Other ghostly figures have been seen including that of a tall monk, dressed in black in the Banquet Hall. He is a friendly ghost and seems to enjoy the great events, which take place in Castle Leslie. Another ghostly figure is that of Sir. Shane's sister who unfortunately drowned herself in the nearby lake.

The Ghosts of Doe Castle, Sheephaven Bay, Co. Donegal

Doe Castle is situated in Sheephaven Bay, N.W. Donegal, near Creeslough and was built in the 15th Century. The name Doe comes from 'na dtuath' meaning 'the territory of the local king'. The castle is a four-storey tower-house which is surrounded by a bawn wall and a moat cut into the rock on the landward side. It was the ancient seat of the Mac Sweeney Chieftains but has changed hands many times over the years and during the 1930s was purchased by the Irish Land Commission and vested as a National Monument.

Doe Castle, Co. Donegal

The tragic tale of Doe Castle is similar to that of Romeo and Juliet and involves the forbidden love of Aileen, the daughter of Maolmhuire and Turlough O'Boyle. The O'Boyle's and the MacSweeney's hated each other. When Aileen's father heard of the romance, he locked Aileen in the top room of the Castle Tower. He then captured Turlough who often went fishing on the Lackagh River in the hope of seeing Aileen.

Turlough was taken back to the Tower and tortured. During the night, he dragged the young O'Boyle to the base of the tree where he killed him with a sword. Unfortunately, Aileen witnessed her lover's death at the hands of her own father and in despair, she jumped to her death from the tower window.

Even today, local fishermen swear that they have seen the phantom boat and the ghosts of two young lovers, smiling and rowing.

Maolmurra – A Ballad of Doe Castle

Wild are thy hills, O Donegal! that frowning darkly rise
As if to greet the mist that falls upon them from the skies:
Dark, dark thy hills, and darker still thy mountain torrents flow,
Yet still more dark Maolmurra's heart in his Castle Hall at Doe.
Fair are thy plains, O Donegal! and calm thy winding streams
Flow gently by each hut and hall, beneath the bright sunbeams;
But plain or stream, or meadow green, or flower upon the lea,
Were not more mild than Maolmurra's child, so sweet and fair was she.
Stout grows thy oak, O Donegal! and straight thy ashen tree,
And swift and strong thy sons so tall, their country's pride to see;
But oak or ash, or young men all, that sprung from Irish soil,
Were not more stout, straight, swift and tall, than the chief of Clan
O'Boyle.
He was the pride of Faugher side, near the hills of Ballymore;
For feats of strength none equaled him from Fanad to Gweedore:
And he would go through frost and snow on the merry Christmas Day
With ringing cheer to hunt the deer from his haunts in dark Glenveigh.
And often in Doe Castle woods he'd hunt the deer and hare,
But the witching deer that drew him there was Maolmurra's daughter
fair;
And there was no man in all the land that trod on Irish soil
Maolmurra's daughter loved so well as Turlogh Og O'Boyle.
In Duntally Wood, as best he could, his love for her he vowed:
But her father, overhearing him, chastised O'Boyle aloud;
With haughty pride, he says: *"Abide by Faugher at the sea,*
For you'll never wed the daughter of Maolmurra of Castle Doe".
In his little boat O'Boyle would float, a-fishing he would go,
With hook and line to Lackagh's stream that runs near Castle Doe;
High in the Castle tower his loved one lay confined,
And on its lofty battlements in sorrow deep she pined.
At the Castle strand two boats lay manned to wait the rising tide,
Maolmurra there in chief command right cowardly did hide;
And when O'Boyle his homeward course steered by the Bishop's Isle,
They there waylaid and a prisoner made of fearless young O'Boyle.

They brought him to the Castle, in strong irons he was bound,
And by Maolmurra was confined in a dungeon underground;
But in a few days after, inside the graveyard wall,
Four stalwart ruffians bore a bier, wrapped in a funeral pall.
Poor Aileen, from the tower high, beheld this mournful scene,
In mute amaze she cast a gaze on the castle graveyard green;
All pale in death, beside a mound of freshly risen soil,
The pall removed, she there beheld the features of O'Boyle.

Then with a shriek she madly leapt from the tower to the ground,
Where by her faithful waiting maid her gory corpse was found;
And in Doe Castle graveyard green, beneath the mouldering soil,
Maolmurra's daughter sleeps in death with Turlogh Og O'Boyle.
And fishers say along the beach a phantom boat does glide
By pale moonlight, at dead of night, there on the silvery tide,
And in that boat two figures sit, upon each face a smile:
They say it is young Aileen fair and Turlogh Og O'Boyle.

**_Song written in the last century by Níall Mac Giolla Brigde from
Feymore, Creeslough._**

Cabra Castle, Kingscourt, Co. Cavan

The original Cabra Castle, owned by the O'Reilly Family, lies in
ruins in Dun Na Rí Forest Park. The current Cabra Castle was built
around 1808 and has changed hands several times. It is now owned
by the Corscadden family.

Cabra Castle was named the second scariest hotel in the world
several years ago by Trip Advisor. There is also a 'Hanging Tree' in
the grounds which is a major attraction to the hotel's many visitors.

Guests of the hotel claim to have experienced apparitions, door
handles rattling and the feeling of being constantly watched. One
visitor claimed to have met a man in an early 20th Century army
uniform striding down one of the corridors. Another guest walked

in on a row about the sale of the castle between – what appeared to be an elderly man and his son.

The saddest ghost story attached to the castle is that of Sarah, who can be heard wailing and crying in what used to be the servant's quarters. Back in the 18th Century, Sarah was one of the servants and had an affair with the owner's son. When she fell pregnant, the owner ordered that she should be killed.

In the middle of the night, she was dragged from her bed and murdered along with her unborn child. Her body was hung from a nearby bridge which is now known as Sarah's Bridge. Her spirit continues to roam the castle and its grounds searching for her child. Some guests have actually heard the sounds of a horse and carriage pull into the courtyard at night and a screaming infant is left at the steps of the hotel. It is then that Sarah stops weeping as her child has been returned.

Cabra Castle, Co. Cavan

Chapter 2
Ghost Searchers Ireland (G.S.I.)

Ghost Searchers Ireland

Ghost Searchers Ireland (G.S.I.) was formed in February 2011 by Caron and Gary Watters and Anne McKinstry. Other team members are Saoirse Campbell, Gavin Heaney, Sarah Monaghan and Karen McCready.

G.S.I.'s main objective is to attempt to find definitive proof of paranormal activity and the existence of spirits. The team are all spiritual and technically minded and very interested in gathering evidence of the super-natural world. Using the most up-to-date equipment to undertake paranormal research, G.S.I. are prepared to travel extensively and have investigated some of the most active locations in Ireland. Some of those locations are covered in this publication and include Ross, Ballygally, Richhill and Shane's Castles. Also Crumlin Road Gaol, Grace Neill's Pub in Donaghadee, The Dobbin's Inn in Carrickfergus, The Crown Bar, Queen Street Police Station and The Cavehill in Belfast, Drumballyroney Church and the Whitehorse Hotel outside Derry.

G.S.I. have also travelled to England to investigate Chillingham Castle and Castle Keep in 2013.

G.S.I. made a fly on the wall documentary for a local network with a local Belfast producer as well as a film made from our experiences at 'Cairndhu House' in Larne titled 'The Last Light'. Back in 2008, Gary and Caron appeared on GMTV on a case of a ghost sighting at the side of the road in Northern Ireland. Further afield the team filmed a pilot show for an American Popular TV network in 2012 and in 2013 an Investigation at Crumlin Road Gaol in Belfast was filmed for Australian TV network on Channel 9. G.S.I. have done a number of charity events for Cancer Research UK, one of which was filmed on Sky TV by the Irish TV network from Duckett's Grove in County Carlow in August 2015.

Gary Watters appeared on the Kevin Smith show in America which goes out live to 50 countries worldwide with 1.5 million viewers.

G.S.I have been interviewed for Ghost Chat Radio and 'Keeping the Spirits Alive' in America, Steve Parsons from 'Most Haunted' on Ghost Chronicles International in the UK and locally with Belfast radio and U105 fm. The team's investigations have featured in many national newspapers around the country and magazines including Paranormal Under Ground in the UK and in America. Many of the G.S.I. investigations are featured on You Tube.

Recording Equipment

To record the paranormal phenomena, G.S.I. use state-of-the-art technical equipment and techniques including the following: - EMF meter, REM Pod, Ultrasound, night vision and thermal cameras. G.S.I. also use live ESP sessions as well as vigil, table tapping, planchette writing and medium contact.

Some Personal Experiences of The Ghost Searchers Ireland Team

My name is Caron Watters. I have been investigating the paranormal along with my husband for over ten years. This story is something that happened when I was about ten years old.

I lived in a haunted house in a well-known haunted estate in Belfast. There was a rumour that the estate was built on a former graveyard. I had a great childhood even though there were lots of stories of things moving all by themselves, people seeing apparitions and hearing all sorts of weird things. One night, a very strange thing happened in my house. My parents had gone for a well-deserved night out and left all seven of us with a babysitter called Jennifer. When they arrived home, there was no babysitter and we were all alone and asleep. This is the story.

My parents departed around 8.00pm and as the children were all asleep, Jennifer made a cup of tea and relaxed in front of the TV, assuming she would have an easy night ahead. It was about 10.30pm that she heard a noise in the kitchen. Thinking that one of the children had wakened and had come down for a drink, she looked inside the kitchen but there was no one there. Confused, she went back into the living room and settled down again. Out of the corner of her eye however, she saw something move in the corner of the living room. It was a ball belonging to one of the children. It then jumped up onto the swivel chair and then the ball came towards her with some force, just missing her head and denting the wall behind. Jennifer then took flight running home and leaving the children behind. She explained later to the children's mother that she would never babysit again in that house.

Personal Experiences by Gary Watters

The Ghost Whisperer

I have been a paranormal investigator for the last twelve years. I have always had an interest in the subject from an experience I had in an old house which dated back to the 1890s in a little town called Donaghadee. When I was twelve, my brother and I shared a large bedroom in the attic overlooking the sea. The house had three storeys and six bedrooms in total.

One summer morning around 5am, I was starting to come out of a sleep but was still lying facing the wall when I started to hear a whisper in my ear. It sounded like it came from an old lady. I automatically thought it was my fourteen old brother messing about so I turned around, quickly ribbed my eyes and noticed that he was still fast asleep in the far side of the bedroom.

At this point, I did not know what was going on so I lay back down again and while fully awake, facing the wall, I heard the old lady whispering in my ear once again but also the cold of her breath! I could not make out what she was saying. I jumped up and looked around the room but there was no one else there apart from my brother who was still fast asleep. I realised that the house could be haunted so I went straight downstairs and lay under my mum and dad's bed until they woke up. I told them what had happened. My brother fell out with me for weeks because I did not wake him up and had left him sleeping in the bedroom all on his own.

Charlie the Ventriloquist Doll

In the same house as the previous story, we used to have an old ventriloquist doll named Charlie. One night my sister and I watched a horror movie on television about such a doll that came to life and murdered people. After watching the horror movie, we going to bed when I noticed that Charlie was sitting upright on one of the dining room chairs. I picked him up and standing on top of a high stool, I reached up and pushed him to the back of a cupboard out of the way. Watching the spooky film about dolls had scared us both.

I closed that cupboard, stood down from the stool and closed the dining room door. My sister and I were about half way up the stairs when we heard a loud bang. We ran down the stairs again and turning on the dining room light, to our horror, Charlie was sitting upright on one of the chairs, staring at my sister and I! To this day, I hate dolls!

Personal Experience By Gavin Heaney

I've always held an interest in the paranormal, but the one incident that got me truly hooked, happened to me when I was in my twenties.

There is a pub in my hometown which I used to visit regularly with my friends. Being a regular, you obviously get to know other customers and have passing acquaintances with some of them. There was a period of several years though where I didn't frequent the pub at all, but one day, I was early for a meeting with some friends, so I sat beside an old man who I had gotten to know from my previous visits several years earlier- we'll call him Jim.

I sat and talked with Jim for a few minutes before excusing myself to use the bathroom. When I came out again, Jim had gone, so not thinking anything of it, I just finished my drink and left to meet my friends.

As chance had it, just a week or so later, I found myself back in the same pub. As I was ordering a drink, the barman joked with me that he hoped I was feeling better this day than I had been on my previous visit. Surprised, I asked him what he meant. He told me that on my last visit, I had sat down at a table in the corner and had started talking to myself. I explained that he was mistaken and I had in fact been talking to Jim. The barman's eyes widened and he proceeded to tell me that Jim had passed away about a year ago......

I recall that my conversation with Jim on that day had just been a general chat – there were no mysterious messages involved. I would also like to state that I was absolutely sober when this happened.

I have never had another experience like this one, but it was definitely the moment that made me realise that there is more to life and death that we will ever know about, and it started me off on my paranormal journey which I feel very privileged to be able to continue with the Ghost Searchers Ireland Team.

Personal Experiences by Saoirse Campbell aka 'Baby Blue'

I have had many personal experiences starting from an early age and there is much to tell. I was just a baby when my parents realised that I was seeing and reacting to something else in the room that could not be seen. As I got older and started to talk, I was able to tell my parents that I could see a man in my bedroom most nights. Things began to escalate and my younger brother and father both began to see the figure also.

The figure had followed my younger brother down the stairs and was seen by my late father who asked my brother to jump. Once he did that, the figure disappeared! My father was so affected by this that he started to freeze and fell down on his hands and knees at the top of the stairs, unable to move. Eventually, he managed to crawl to his bedroom and pulled himself onto the bed until the freezing feeling left him.

Windows all over the house started to rattle and rumble as if somebody was violently banging on them. This was witnessed by others as well. There were many other banging noises heard all through the house. I also had an out of body experience one night at home. Whatever was causing all these manifestations appeared to be focusing on me!

After nine years of living in this house, we finally moved out. However, this was not the end and activity continued on in our next house. When I was old enough, I moved out into my own accommodation but no matter where I went, I would experience all sorts of different things. Later, I had my own kids and in one house, the toys would move by themselves, baby wipes flew off the table and my shower door would bang shut. At least three spirits were seen not just by myself but others who came to visit.

I am now living in a new development for almost two years and things have started kicking off here too! Doors have been heard slamming, footsteps heard in the halls and lights have been turning on and off. I have also heard whispering in my ear but also my partner has experienced the same thing.

I have had so many experiences in my life that I have basically learned to live with them. All of these inspired me to take the matter further and join the most amazing paranormal team in Ireland, namely Ghost Searchers Ireland (G.S.I.). I really enjoy the work and I get a real adrenaline rush from it. It is such an intriguing hobby to have and so many people are interested in it.

I can remember my first paranormal investigation with G.S.I. –

definitely one to remember in Crumlin Road Gaol and before I joined G.S.I. I was only a follower at that time and decided to act brave and enter a cell on my own with the door closed over. After around five to ten minutes, I could hear something shuffling, as if someone was pacing up and down the cell. I began to fell physically sick! I was escorted out of the cell and into the main hall where I was given a drink. After half an hour, I still had not improved and I left the premises but was actually sick outside the door. That dreadful feeling passed almost immediately. Could I have been affected by a spirit of a prisoner? Who knows!

I followed G.S.I. for almost a year before I became a trainee and then a full-time investigator. I have experienced so much and still carve for more. I have added further stories of my experiences at Queen Street Police Station (page 73) and also Donaghadee Old Town Hall (see opposite).

G.S.I. have been to numerous locations, some that we find ourselves returning to. We come away with amazing results which we share with the public either by going live on social media or recording it and posting on You Tube or our Facebook page.

Personal Experience By Sarah Monaghan

One of my first ever paranormal investigations was in an Athenaeum in Enniscorthy in County Wexford. It stands out for me as I caught a class A EVP (electronic voice phenomenon). We were underneath the stage of the Theatre and we were carrying out an EVP session. We had a medium with us who had picked up on the spirit of a man called Stephen who the medium had said had come in from Enniscorthy Castle next door to the Athenaeum to have a nosey. I had hit record on the voice recorder and the medium called out, *"Stephen are you here with us?"* Then there was a long, silent pause. The medium then continued, *"Stephen, I know you are here with us, can you make a noise for us as I know you have the strength to do it?"* then there was another long, silent pause.

I stopped the recording to play it back and we were all amazed with what the recording had picked up. During the medium's first question, *"Stephen, are you here with us?"* there is a man's voice that says, *"Yes I am.........hello?"* Then during the second question when the medium asks for Stephen to make a noise you can clearly hear 3 knocks. This undoubtedly is one of the best pieces of evidence I have ever caught of the paranormal as I know how silent it was during the recording and how clear the man's voice comes through when we played it back.

Personal Experiences by Karen McCready

The Man in Donaghadee

Nestled in the beautiful seaside town of Donaghadee, on the coast of County Down lies Donaghadee Old Town Hall. It was built in the 1770s and was once a bustling family home before it became the Harbour Office and then the Town Hall. It now lies silent and derelict.

Deciding that I should brave this three storey building, with only its spirits for company, I set off on a 'lone vigil' which I would stream live on Facebook.

Some of the equipment I had taken with me included a 'Coultous Box', a type of ghost box or spirit box, as they are more commonly known. Setting this up in one of the large downstairs rooms (which we refer fondly as the 'safe room' due to the fact that the safe is located there), I began an initial walk around. Having set up further equipment over the next two floors and making sure that the building was empty, I returned to the lower level to begin my live-streamed 'lone vigil'.

A spirit or ghost box can scan through the radio stations at a fast speed, generally only landing on each station for about a quarter of a second. Therefore, to get a full recognisable word, particularly, as an intelligent response to a question asked is exciting. Anything more than two words is uncommon and as you can imagine, a full sentence is incredibly rare.

I began with the standard introductions myself, stated my reasons for being there, and encouraged any spirits within the building to come out of the shadows and to use this device as a means of communication with me. During these questions, I could hear knocks and bangs and what sounded like footsteps coming from the stairs and the floor above. Deciding that perhaps I should continue my investigation elsewhere, I asked, *"Do you want me to go out onto the stairs? do you want me to go into another room?"*. Very quickly, a male voice with a distinct Northern Irish accent came the reply *"come halfway up the stairs…!"* Which of course I did…

Some more places in Ulster where the G.S.I. Team have carried out Investigations.

Many of the following can be seen on the Ghost Searchers Ireland You Tube Channel.

Ram's Island Haunting, Lough Neagh

Ram's Island is located in Lough Neagh. Legend has it that it has a strong connection with the Fae or Fairy people. The G.S.I. team carried out an investigation on the island around eight years ago.

After a ten-minute boat trip from the shore to the Island, we set up camp on the upper level of the island. That night the team was sitting around the camp when dusk was setting in when all ten of us saw a figure walk around the camp and then disappear off the edge which was quite a large drop. Initially, we thought that someone else was on the island apart from ourselves. We, almost immediately all run over to the spot where the figure had disappeared but to our shock, there was no one was there. We also checked all the pathways to no avail.

After returning to the camp we split into two teams. Four of the investigators were doing a vigil about five minutes from the camp. Everyone was standing silent when we all heard a massive bang as if something had fallen out of a tree. The noise almost sounded like a person had just jumped from the tree behind us, but no one was there. We had no explanation to what this sound was. Near the end of the investigation two of the ladies was sitting around the camp when they heard what sounded like footsteps walking around them. They switched on their torches as there was not enough light to see anything from the campfire. To their horror there was no one there. The rest of the group had long gone down to the other side of the Island.

The Copeland Islands, Co. Down

Back in August 2013, the G.S.I. team had the pleasure to travel across to the Copeland Islands in Strangford Lough. The Copeland Islands are around fifteen minutes by boat from Donaghadee. On arrival we decided to pitch up tent beside the only graveyard on the island. We waited until dark and decided to split up into two teams. Team 1 investigated the graveyard and Team 2 went to the other side of the island where there was a cave system. While Team 1 carried out a vigil down in the graveyard, some of the team experienced a feeling of been touched on the arm and one team member saw something darting in and out of the gravestones. They went to investigate and found no one, however, they got strange readings on their equipment especially when the temperature dropped within seconds.

Team 2 were half way across the island when they all saw a strange light in the wooded area of the island. On inspection they could not find any natural source of the strange pulsating light, which was very bizarre. The next day everyone was waiting for the boat and within two minutes a fast mist appeared like a scene from

'The Fog'. The mist seemed to last forever. When we heard the boat coming in, we were very relieved and glad to get off the island. When speaking to the captain, he said he had not seen a mist like that before come and go so quickly and he had been boating for over twenty years!

The Ghost House, Newry, Co. Down

Some time ago the G.S.I. team had the opportunity of visiting a rural, long forgotten cottage outside Newry. The cottage was once a home of a World War I solder and it is said that he continues to haunt his former home as well as another spirit who is not so nice.

The last tenants of the cottage were a family who fled the building with just the clothes on their backs. After they took down religious relics off the walls, the family left all the rest of their worldly possessions behind and never looked back. The reason for their quick departure was lot of poltergeist activity in the cottage.

The G.S.I. team set up for the nights investigation and then prepared all their ghost haunting equipment including laser grids, locked off cameras, and EPS recorders, etc. The investigators decided to start off with a seance in the kitchen area and had a laser grid pointed down the hallway from just outside the kitchen area. A couple of hours into our investigation we decided to go back into the kitchen and hold hands for energy and a 'call out'. There were about seven-eight investigators in the cottage and no one else.

The team started to hear strange sounds coming from upstairs, then as if someone was walking along the landing. One of the investigators went up the stairs to see if maybe someone had accidentally wandered in during the evening but returned saying there was no one there.

The team stood still and listened for a few moments when they heard a man's voice coming from the living room. Once again an investigator went to have a look, but as before, there was no one there. Remembering that the laser grid was set up to look down the hall, the team looked at the recording and were astounded to see what looked like half of a body from the waist down turning from the corner of the kitchen and walk down the hall way.

This was the first time some of the team had ever seen anything like this.

Several investigators saw the same thing, one actually commented that they had seen the full apparition of a man coming from the corner of the kitchen and turn to continue walking down the hallway. The team went back a few times to see if the same phenomena would happen again, but unfortunately it did not.

Other strange phenomena happened during the visit to the cottage. Earlier on in the day, just as the team arrived, there was a horse roaming around the cottage. It was quite friendly and let the team pet him but suddenly the horse was spooked by something and it sped off down the laneway. The cattle in the nearby field did the same thing.

The team also conducted a ghost box session in the room which would have been the living room. A ghost box is a piece of equipment that scans up and down the radio waves and it is believed that ghosts/spirits can use the white noise in between to communicate with the living. A member of the team walked away to look out in the hall when a voice came over the ghost box saying the name of the investigator demanding her to come back to the area where the rest of the team was. Did the ghost not want the investigator to look out at the hallway as fear of being seen again? Between seeing apparitions walking down the hall and hearing footsteps upstairs the team was in no doubt this cottage was haunted.

Donaghadee Town Hall, Co. Down

The Town Hall in Donaghadee is a three-storey house built in the 1770s. Running down the side of the building is a lane, once known as 'Murder Lane'.

The G.S.I. team have carried out a number of investigations at this location and their recordings can be seen on YouTube. A number of strange phenomena were observed by the team including the name 'Matthew' which came through on the voice recorder. Matthew was disabled and kept in the cellar away from the public eye. His 'minder' or 'the key keeper' also came through.

Members of the public also participated in several of the visits with funds raised for the charity Cancer Research UK. The name 'Thomas' also came through the live EVP. During a table tapping session where there were seven people sitting around a folding table with their fingers touching, the table began to move!

Donaghadee Town Hall (Courtesy of G.S.I)

Carrickmacross Workhouse, Co. Monaghan

Built in 1841 during the Famine, this workhouse was one of many built to accommodate the destitute people of the area. Originally built to house five hundred people, at one time there were around two thousand inhabitants.

The G.S.I. team came here in 2014 and visited a number of the sections of the workhouse. A number of children came through with one stating he had been murdered and buried in the grounds outside. Caron actually saw a figure and felt the presence of a little boy. While in the kitchen, the team heard a massive crash but there was no other persons in the building. Some figures were also noticed by the team including one going past one of the windows and then outside near the former gravesite. Stones were also thrown in the graveyard.

Benburb Priory, Co. Tyrone

The earliest building here would date from the 16th Century and the ruins of the Castle are located in the grounds. Benburb Priory was once used as a military hospital during WW11 and then as a training centre for young priests run by the Servites. It now holds an extensive library and museum as well as the O'Neill Collection relating to the O'Neill clans of Ulster.

Benburb Priory

The Ghost Searchers Ireland team visited here recently and picked up quite a lot of activity in the building. Footsteps were heard in the corridor and the cellar but no one was there and when playing back the voice recorder, the team heard a sigh or a whisper and the word 'go'. Using the 'ghost box', the question was asked about the names of the priests who had lived here. A voice came through saying *"Chris"*.

When the question was asked, *"What was your rank in the military during the war?"*, a male voice replied, *"regiment"*.

On another occasion the name 'Sean O'Neill' came through on the ghost box. The O'Neill Clan has a rich history in the Benburb area.

Chapter 3
Other Haunted Buildings

Crumlin Road Gaol, Belfast

Crumlin Road Gaol or 'the Crum' as it is commonly known dates from the Victorian era and is situated in North Belfast, a short distance from Belfast City Centre. Built between 1843 and 1845, it was used as a prison up to March 1996 and was officially closed in 1998. Around 25,000 people were imprisoned here and at least seventeen were executed within its walls. Many of the latter were buried within the walls of the prison in graves marked only by their initials.

Some of the earlier occupants included children who were imprisoned for petty offences including stealing food. More recent famous prisoners included the late Ian Paisley and Martin McGuinness.

The former gaol is home to a number of ghosts and many ghost hunters and visitors have experienced strange phenomena including noises, voices, touching and even sightings both day and night. The building is now a major tourist attraction and holds a

Crumlin Road Gaol (Courtesy of G.S.I.)

C-Wing was home to the famous 'Condemned Man's Cell' and is said to be the one of the most haunted parts of the Gaol. The drop-cell in the basement where the condemned man hangs until he is confirmed dead is another spooky place.

Another part of the site is an underground tunnel which runs from the Gaol under the Crumlin Road to the former Courthouse and which was used to transport criminals between the two buildings. Even when it was an active prison, wardens would report strange goings on inside the tunnel and today a grey figure is often seen here. Michael Wallace who is one of the editors of this book also had an experience in the tunnel. Michael was on one of the paranormal tours of the Gaol which are ran every Halloween. Whilst on the tour the tour guide asked for a volunteer to walk across the tunnel and back which Michael agreed. When he was walking along there was a huge bang on a door and no one else was there.

B-Wing houses 'the padded cell' which is another haunted section of the gaol. Visitors have felt very uneasy in the cell, they have been touched or pushed while there and many have seen a dark figure lurking in the corner of the cell. A dark figure has also been seen wandering around both B-Wing and in D-Wing. One such figure has been seen standing in the doorways watching the visitors as they pass through. He is said to be a former warden, who although dead for many years, still likes to keep an eye on the prison.

One of the many ghosts is that of an American Jew who was hanged here for a crime that he did not commit, his ghost still can be seen walking through the corridors and iron walkways. Another ghost is that of a young boy, Patrick Magee, who rather than be hanged, committed suicide at the age of thirteen years. He would have cried himself to sleep in the prison and those cries can still be heard from time to time during the night. Other ghosts include former wardens who were employed in the gaol.

One story involved a group of friends who were walking through the tunnel which connects the prison to the courthouse across the road. It is a cold dark clammy place and the wind blows through it. One of the group felt that he was being watched. As the rest of the group walked, two of them stood back to look at something that had caught their eye earlier. But nothing was there and when they turned around to rejoin the group, all they could see was darkness. What appeared to be a child's voice called out behind them, *"Come play with us"*. They then heard children laughing and giggling but they could see nothing. Panicking, they ran but could still hear the voice, *"Come play with us"*. One turned around to see a small arm stretched towards him but there was nothing else! He screamed and ran faster to join the group again. The friends still think of their strange experience in the tunnel and have been unable to explain it.

Another strange tale concerns a visitor to the jail who lay down in a coffin for a photograph and when it was developed, there was an image of a strange face next to his!

Ghost Searchers Ireland (G.S.I.) Investigations at Crumlin Road Gaol

Shadows by Gavin Heaney (G.S.I.)

My first experience as a team member with G.S.I. at Crumlin Road Gaol occurred on Friday the 13th! We were escorting members of the public around the gaol on one of our four-hour paranormal investigations. While carrying out table-tapping and automatic writing experiments with members of the public in Lower D-Wing, I noticed a strange shadow moving rapidly from side to side across the dimly lit doorway which leads into the bowels of D-Wing. I approached the doorway to investigate further to see if I could find a logical explanation for the shadow. As I got to within fifteen feet of the doorway, I kneeled down just to give myself a different perspective. It was on this approach, that the shadow either seemed to stop moving-or perhaps disappear altogether.

That turned out to be my mistaken opinion because as I sat there watching, a very dense, pitch, black shadow then came rocketing out of the doorway towards me with incredible speed - as if it had stated at the back of the Wing and had built up energy and speed as it came towards me. When it got to within about six feet of me, the shadow suddenly dissipated and disappeared- as if whatever it was had suddenly run out of energy. I stayed in the same position for at least another twenty-thirty seconds, stunned and speechless as to what had happened.

I remain convinced to this day, that if I had been close to the doorway, whatever it was that had launched itself at me, would have had enough energy and force to physically knock me over - as I have seen tables being pushed forcefully into people in exactly the same area of the prison.

There are lots of restless spirits in the gaol - most of which are probably very angry and obviously capable of being very strong when they feel the need to lash out at the living. I still have no rational explanation for what happened on this night - and despite my many subsequent experiences in Crumlin Road Gaol, this one remains the one that has made me feel the most uneasy.

However, it is also one of the reasons why the gaol will always be my favourite location to investigate.

Touched by Unseen Hands by Gavin Heaney (G.S.I.)

The G.S.I. (Team Blue) are in the fortunate position of currently being the only paranormal investigation team to be allowed access to the Crumlin Road Gaol in Belfast- a fact that we never take for granted and which we are always extremely grateful for, as the prison is one of the premier locations anywhere in Ireland.

Being trusted friends of the gaol, we are occasionally granted permission to conduct 'team only' investigations after the building has been closed for the day and no one else is inside. On one of these team only investigations, which we were filming for our You Tube Channel, I was on Upper B wing with two other team members. As I was filming using a night vision camcorder, I took up position just outside a toilet block, and as were calling out to the spirits, I was touched on the back of my neck by unseen hands. It was as if someone had run their finger from the back of my head and right down my neck. There was of course, no living person standing behind me when this happened.

Just shortly after this, as we were making our way down Upper B towards the Circle, I had a set of old iron keys with me that I used as a possible trigger object. As I was walking along Upper B, I was rattling these keys and calling out-saying that I was a new prison officer and I was going to lock them all up. As I stood in front of an open cell, I then felt the second touch which I experienced that night. This time, it felt as if someone had run their hands quite slowly right across the top of my back starting at my left shoulder and finishing at my right. When it reached my right shoulder, I then experienced an unpleasant smell-as if someone with very bad breath had breathed into my face.

Had I antagonised a spirit with my pretend claim to be a guard? Or had something-or someone-from just a few minutes earlier followed me down the wing from the toilet area? Who knows? But it is experiences like these-along with all the other unseen touches and the many voices we hear giving intelligent responses through our various ghost boxes which keep me addicted to paranormal investigation.

The Ghost Boy in Crumlin Road Gaol by Sarah Monaghan (G.S.I.)

It was All Hallows' Eve at one of the most haunted gaols in Ireland, The Crumlin Road Gaol. Two fellow paranormal investigators and myself were in the gaol's hospital all night. We were carrying out Ghost Box sessions with the public who were arriving in groups about every thirty minutes or so. The hospital wing was candle lit, cold and the perfect place for a Halloween scare. We were waiting for the next group to arrive when I saw a brown haired boy who looked about thirteen years standing behind the entrance of the wing as if he was too shy to enter. I shouted, *"Oh! Come on in!"*. My two teammates both turned to me and said, *"Who are you talking to?"* I said, *"The boy...."*, looking back to the entrance I realised there was no one there. I had not seen any physical evidence of ghosts until that night in the darkness of Crumlin Road Gaol.

The Changing Rooms at Crumlin Road Gaol by Karen McCready (G.S.I.)

As part of G.S.I.'s four-hour paranormal tour of this really historical location, we are able to take members of the public into the Changing Rooms of the Gaol. These changing rooms were one of the first places the prisoners were taken and placed into one of the small individual cubicles, asked to strip off their personal clothes and given prison issued ones.

Gary, another team member and myself had a group of around fourteen people in this changing room conducting what we call an EVP session. (Electronic Voice Phenomenon where a simple recording device is used).

The members of the public stood in a circle, each asked a question, and a pause of about fifteen to twenty seconds was left between. We asked everyone else to be as silent as possible throughout the experiment so that we could playback and hear any answers to the questions on the voice recorder.

With only the moonlight coming in through a few of the top windows, I heard footsteps very clearly coming from the corner of the room. I was about to 'tag it', (a phrase that is used when someone shuffles their feet, coughs or moves so that we can later debunk that noise). I was so convinced that it must have been one of the people in front of me, as it was so clear. However, when I looked around quietly at everyone's feet, I could see that no one was moving. So I said nothing in the hope of catching the noise on the recording.

I continued silently around the inside of the circle of people, recording the various questions asked and there was no other sound. We finished and gathered to hear the recording, plugging in a speaker to help hear any low whispers. When the recording began, the footsteps that I had heard in real-time, were clearly audible. The two people who had been in front of me stated that they had also heard these same footsteps coming from behind them. They reconfirmed that neither of them had moved their own feet.

We continued listening to the recording of the questions but there was only silence afterwards. By this time, apart from the footsteps, I felt sure we had not managed to catch any EVP's. The last question was asked by one of the males in the group, *"Are you male or female?"* and in a very clear but rushed female whisper, the answer came back, *"Female"*.

Every single person in the room heard this reply and Gary and I gasped at how clear it was. I am not afraid to admit that I felt goose bumps on my arms as I also remembered the footsteps (heels?), which were heard so clearly walking around the room earlier.

Armagh Gaol, Co. Armagh

The Gaol was closed in 1986 but has a long history with many tales of murder, suicides and tortures. In the 1700s, there were many gruesome stories of cruelty and prisoners crammed into the tiny cells. Executions also took place in Gaol Square and then behind the Prison Walls and it is said that many of the bodies were hacked into pieces and scattered around Armagh although some were buried in the prison grounds. Many of the prisoners were interred for minor crimes or no crimes at all. It was originally designed as a women only prison but extended in the mid 1800s to include debtors and felons. During the 'Troubles' it held many high-profile political prisoners. One of the prison officers, Agnes Wallace was shot dead in the gaol in 1979.

Armagh Gaol, Co. Armagh

It has a reputation of being haunted and shadowy figures have been seen moving around the deserted building. Ghostly faces have also been seen looking out of the windows. Paranormal investigators have visited the premises and have reported strange phenomena. On one such visit, all the phone batteries started to drain so that the investigators were unable to take photos.

The Raholp Funeral Ghost, Co. Down

Raholp comes from 'Ráth Cholpa' meaning 'fort of the steer' and is a townland situated 5.5km North East of Downpatrick. Some two hundred years ago, a man from Raholp, outside Downpatrick died. His family held the usual wake and funeral for him although they were not sorry to see him go, as he was a tyrant and had made their lives miserable. As the funeral cortege was leaving his former home on its way to the nearby cemetery, the mourners were shocked and dismayed to see the face of the deceased staring out from one of his windows. It appeared that he was laughing at his own funeral!

The mourners were thrown into confusion and scattered. Even the funeral horses bolted in fright. Eventually, the funeral started out again but the horses would not budge no matter how hard the undertaker tried. It was suggested that he use a donkey to pull the hearse. This worked and his remains reached the cemetery. However, the deceased was buried in an unmarked grave.

His wife and daughter lived contentedly for a number of years until one night while saying their prayers; they heard an unearthly laugh coming from the walls of the house. Suddenly the ghost of the old man appeared and he proceeded to laugh at them until dawn the next day. The same horrible haunting continued each night until they decided to call in the local priest to help them. The priest felt overwhelmed by his task and felt he needed to get some help and indeed several priests attended the exorcism. They all noticed a strange unearthly atmosphere when they entered the house.

The exorcism began with the priests calling out for the old man to appear. After the third attempt, the spectre revealed itself. The priests placed a bottle on the floor and then continued the exorcism by saying a number of prayers and sprinkling the room with holy water. Finally, the spirit was forced into the bottle but not before it let out one last mocking screech. The bottle was quickly sealed, taken out of the house and hidden beneath an old mill wheel where it was destined to remain undisturbed for one hundred years.

That period of time has now passed and some local people have claimed to have seen the ghost of the old man as he searches for his former home.

Drumbeg Manor, Inver, Co. Donegal

Inver lies between Killybegs and Donegal Town. The name Drumbeg is derived from 'An Droim Beag' meaning 'the little ridge'.

Drumbeg Manor is said to be among the most haunted houses in the whole of Europe with numerous reports of hauntings and not a place for the faint hearted! Some people have heard a screaming woman in the manor while others have claimed to have seen a man dressed in a white suit who roams the corridors of this dwelling.

Lissan House, Co. Tyrone

Lissan House lies outside Cookstown and is over 400 years old and previously owned by the Staples family. The paintings of Sir Robert Ponsonby Staples (1853-1943) still hang in the hallway. He was quite eccentric and would often walk around in his bare feet and was therefore known as the 'Barefoot Baronet'.

The last of the family was Hazel Radcliffe Dolling and she often heard strange noises throughout the house including heavy male footsteps at night. Others have heard a child crying at night even though there were no children present. The house contains many cold spots and often the aroma of rose petals and lavender hang about the air. One visitor came upon a group of children playing in the first floor landing. When she called out to them, they ignored her and then ran off down the hall before completely disappearing.

Lissan House, Co. Tyrone

Ardglass Golf Club, Co. Down

The clubhouse of Ardglass Golf Club is one of the oldest clubhouse buildings in the world and dates from the 18th century but the warehouses in the grounds date from 1400 and Horn Castle near the first tee dates from 1377.

Like all very old towns and buildings, Ardglass has its share of ghosts and other strange tales. The ghost of a 'grey lady' has been seen passing through the club house walls where there used to be doors. In the bar, patrons have reported hearing snooker being played but the noise comes from an empty room upstairs, which used to be the snooker room. When some renovations were being carried out in 1927, workmen unearthed the skeletal remains of a young child in the wall cavity within the clubhouse. An inquest had to be carried out before its burial in one of the local graveyards.

Ardglass Golf Club, Co. Down

Grace Neill's Public House, Co. Down

Grave Neill's is located in Donaghadee, Co. Down and is best known as the oldest pub in Ireland. The pub first opened in 1611 and was called the 'King's Arms'. It was renamed 'Grace Neill's' in the 20th Century after its previous landlady who would greet all of her customers with a kiss on the cheek. The pub was a wedding present given to Grace by her father and she ran this welcoming establishment for many years. She was quite a character, puffing on a clay pipe as she watched proceedings. She died in 1916 at the age of 98 years.

Grace's ghost still lives on in the pub and is often seen in the front bar, dressed in Victorian style clothing, where she tidies the glasses. Shuffling and creaking floorboards have been heard on the second floor by both staff and customers. Some people have felt 'an invisible presence' pass through them in the vicinity of the pub's staircase and the strong smell of pipe smoke wafts around the bar even though smoking has been banned inside for many years.

Despite all this ghostly activity, the present landlord is keen to point out that customers have nothing to fear from Grace.

Dobbin's Inn Hotel, Carrickfergus

The Dobbin's Inn has a long and carried history and was once used as a gaol when it was an old police barracks. The oldest part of the building dates from the 13th Century and there is a 'priest's hole' in the reception. It is also claimed that the building was once connected to the nearby castle by a tunnel.

Dobbin's Inn, Carrickfergus

A story is told that Maud (Elizabeth) the wife of one of the 17th Century commanders of Carrickfergus Castle had an affair with a soldier called 'Button Cap' from the nearby castle. When her husband discovered the deceit, he murdered both of them. Her ghost still appears in the Reception area and has been known to stroke the faces of visitors, as they are asleep. She has also been seen disappearing into one of the big chimneybreast and re-appearing on the other side.

The G.S.I. Team carried out an investigation at the Dobbin's Inn Hotel back in 2011. When they were carrying out a seance, a female calling herself Elizabeth identified herself to the team. Elizabeth also made her presence felt by stroking the faces of the team. Some of the G.S.I. team members noticed shadows and movement in the corner of the room as well as the noise of a lady's dress swishing past them. During the Franks Box session, the team was spoken to in French and another being told the team to 'get out' quite aggressively.

The Crown Bar, Belfast

Like many other old public houses, the famous Crown Bar in Great Victoria Street in Belfast has its own ghost. Amelia was a former prostitute who fell down the stairs breaking her neck.

The Crown Bar, Belfast

The Abercorn Arms, Newtownstewart, Co. Tyrone

Back in 1883, the Newry Reporter described a ghostly tale from this hotel.

One night a family from England arrived to stay a few hours until their coach was ready to depart in the early hours the next morning. They were all given rooms to sleep in including their governess. However, she was accommodated in an attic room away from the rest of the guests. Saying that she was frightened to be on her own, she demanded that one of the servants stay with her in a make-up bed. She was described as a tall distinguished lady with a fantastic head of hair, which was pinned up high on her head with curls reaching down her neck.

They settled in for the night and the maid remarked that the governess did not unpin her hair before she went to sleep. The governess appeared to have a disturbed night and kept asking if it was time to get up. The maid reassured her that the night watchman would waken her but eventually decided to go down to check the time downstairs. It was just after midnight and when the maid ascended the stairs she put her foot on what appeared to be a great shaggy dog. She gently kicked it out of her way and then she noticed that the shape was in fact an old man! Showing a toothless mouth, he cried, *"in her hair"*. Just at that time the night watchman also appeared and shouted, *"Great God! What's that?"* The maid flew up the stairs to the bedroom and the shape also disappeared.

The maid just about reached the governess's bed before she fainted. The governess then screamed and awoke the whole house.

Eventually, Rose, the maid was able to tell her story including the old man's words *"in her hair"*. At this, the governess screamed again and put her hands to her head as if to hold in position her massive coils of hair. All went quiet again and they managed to get some sleep before departing early the next morning.

Rose and the night watchman were convinced that they had seen a ghost and also that it was connected in some way with the governess. They told their story many times and it spread far and wide even attracting more visitors to the Abercorn Arms in the prospect of seeing the ghost for themselves. Another English visitor then arrived and stayed there for a week. He was very interested in all the stories around the area and seemed to enjoy talking with everybody. No one knew that secretly, he was taking notes.

Later on, a friend of the owner of the Abercorn Arms sent him a letter and a newspaper cutting describing the trial for a theft of jewels of a Miss Hemmerton, a governess in the Hepburn family. This was the same governess who had stayed in the hotel.

The story described that in a previous employment, she had worked for an elderly gentleman in Scotland. He had amassed a fortune while in India and had invested in some precious jewels. She had actually witnessed the old man with his box of jewels and knew where he had hid them. As time went on, he suffered a stroke and was unable to communicate. When he died, his papers indicated that after a period of six months, his case was to be opened and it would reveal the jewels. However, when it was opened, it was empty.

Some members of his family believed that the old man was hallucinating but others were convinced that the story was true and the jewels had gone missing. Suspicion fell on his former employee, Miss Hemmerton, who had left and moved to Ireland. A private detective was employed to investigate that matter. When she was traced, she appeared to be above suspicion and it was only when he tracked her movements to the Abercorn Arms and he heard the story of the ghost, that he was convinced that she was actually concealing the missing jewels in her hair!

Confronted with this new evidence, the governess then made a full confession. After the old man had died, she became terrified of being left alone at night, it seemed that the little old man was haunting her for the return of his jewels. The episode in the Abercorn Arms only made her more terrified as the description of the person seen on the stairs was exactly that of her previous employer.

The newspaper reported that she was then sentenced to penal servitude. As for Rose and the night watchman, they were relieved that their ghost story was believed as true after all. Life then settled back to normal at the Abercorn Arms.

The Barracks, Ballyshannon, Co. Donegal

Stories exist of a lady in a green silk dress who caused fear and death to anyone who seen her. One such tale involved a young soldier who was so smitten with the lady that he abandoned his post. On realizing his error and that the lady was actually the ghost of a general's daughter who had died some time ago, it was too late!

His crime of abandoning his post was discovered and he was later executed!

Haunted Police Station, Queen Street, Belfast

Built in the 1870s, the building was once a children's hospital and then became a police barracks and is widely known for being haunted. Many unexplained things have happened there over the years in its maze of corridors and rooms. Ghost Searchers Ireland decided to visit the site and spend the night in it. What happened that night was quite peculiar.

Some of the investigators were in one of the former holding cells and were using several pieces of monitoring equipment. Contact was made with a child and also a member of the armed forces who had worked there at one time. Lots of noises were also heard by the team including what appeared to be the radiators rattling.

The second team were located in a room where all the walls were painted black with quotes written in chalk. The team sensed a very bad atmostphere here and something lurking in the corners. At one stage the team were told to *'get out'* when a voice came through on the Franks Box. On another visit, other 'beings' came through including a lady and a Detective who had worked in the building. The G.S.I. team concluded that this was indeed a very spooky building!

Sharon Rectory, Newtowncunningham, Co. Donegal

This rectory is associated with a double murder, which took place at the end of the 18th Century. One of the murder victims was

Mrs. Waller and her spirit is said to haunt the dwelling. Also known as the 'Blue Lady', she would appear every night. The murder story involved Dr. William Hamilton, a local magistrate and clergyman who had to shelter in the manor, as he was unable to get a ferry across Lough Swilly due to the bad weather.

This was during the Irish Rebellion era and it was decided to ambush the magistrate on his way home. When the United Irishmen arrived they demanded that Hamilton be handed over to them and this was refused. Mrs. Waller ran to guard her husband who was an invalid while Dr. Hamilton hid beside her. When the attackers fired their guns through the window, Mrs. Waller was mortally wounded. Dr. Hamilton hid in the cellar and once again refused to come outside. The servants, very angry and also scared of their fate managed to get him upstairs but he held on to the banisters. A hot poker was then used on his hands and he was then thrown outside the door where he was also killed. He lay all night on the stone and it is said that the latter was taken to Trinity College, Dublin, as his blood would still appear on it. The attackers were very annoyed by their actions when they heard of Mrs. Waller, as the lady was very well liked in the area. Apparently, her spirit and that of the magistrate still haunt the rectory.

Springhill House, Moneymore, Co. Derry

There are a number of ghosts linked with this manor house, now managed by the National Trust, which was built over three hundred years ago by 'Good-Will' Conynghan.

The main ghost is that of Olivia Lennox Conynghan, the widow of Colonel Conynghan, an army officer. While he was away, he heard that his children were very ill with smallpox. He abandoned his post and came home but later faced a court-marshal. Although his family survived, one of his daughters later died. Colonel Conynghan became very depressed and suicidal. One particular night, his wife, sensing he was about to take his life, rushed to his room but she was too late!

It is claimed that her ghost has been seen at the top of the oak staircase, raising her arms in despair as she rushes to the same room before it fades away. She is known, however, as a friendly ghost and loves to see visitors to her former home. Her ghost been seen standing over the children of the house as they sleep. Once satisfied that they are safe, she disappears again.

Another story concerns a visitor who was staying in the Blue Room in Springhill House. She awoke to see a group of agitated servants in the room as well as the spirit of someone coming out of a door behind her to calm them down. The visitor eventually fell asleep but in the morning realised that there was no door where the spirit had entered the room the night before. At breakfast, she mentioned what had happened and was told that there was indeed a door there but it had been papered over.

Some years later, the door was re-opened to reveal a powder closet. There was an old pair of gloves and a small pouch which contained some bullets lying on the floor. Within the Blue Room, objects are known to move around even though no one has been inside and some items have completely disappeared. A grey lady has been seen in the Cedar room where she touches the occupants.

Gillhall, Dromore, Co. Down

One of the most famous ghost stories in Ireland comes from the Gillhall Estate on the Lurgan Road just outside Dromore. At one time, this estate consisted of a manor built around 1680, farm houses and land.

The future Lord Tyrone and his cousin the future Lady Beresford were raised as orphans here during the 17th Century. Their 'tutor' was a 'deist' and believed that God created the universe but left it to natural change and evolution with no need for organised religion. The two children followed this belief and even made a pact that of either of them should die, that person would return from the dead and provide proof that they were indeed dead and also the existence of an afterlife.

Some years later, Lady Beresford was wakened from her sleep only to find the ghost of Lord Tyrone by her bedside. He told her that he had died that day and had now fulfilled his promise to return from the next world. He also told her that she would have a son and that her first husband would die young and that she would remarry. However, he also added a chilling forecast that she would die herself on her 47th birthday. As proof of his visit, he grabbed her wrist and left a very bad burn scar. After that, he disappeared. Lady Beresford always hid the scar with a ribbon tied around her wrist.

GILLHALL, DROMORE, CO. DOWN.

Very soon after this event, news of Lord Tyrone's death reached Gillhall and over the years all of his prophecies came through except for the last one as Lady Beresford lived beyond her 47th birthday. She decided to hold a party and invited many of her old friends including the vicar who had baptised her as a baby. When he arrived, he wished her a happy 47th birthday – he had checked the church records before coming to Gillhall. The family were all surprised that Lady Beresford was actually one year younger than she thought. However, she herself was dismayed as she remembered her cousin's prophecy that she would die on her 47th birthday.

She then told her son and the rest of the family all the details and after making provisions for her family's future, she retired to bed and died within the hour! Later, the family removed the black ribbon from her wrist and found the scarred flesh left by the hand of the ghost of Lord Tyrone.

Over the years since her death, many ghost stories came out of Gillhall. When the 5th Earl of Clanwilliam brought his new bride there in 1909, she found the presence of the ghost too much to bear and the house was abandoned shortly afterwards.

Although, there was a manager and his family residing in a part of the house for some years, it eventually was deserted and it fell into disrepair. It was destroyed by a fire in 1969 and had to be demolished. However, the ghostly legend of Gillhall lives on and people are known to pass the gates as quickly as possible for fear of seeing the infamous ghost.

Flax House, Belfast

This building consists of five stories and was built in 1912 when the linen industry was thriving in Belfast. The mill workers were mostly women and they had to work long hours in harsh conditions. The mill closed in 1966 and a printing company moved in in the 1990s. Soon after its employees started to notice very strange happenings- doors would open and close by themselves and the temperature in the building would suddenly drop. There was also the sound of women shouting and singing and then ghostly figures of women were seen throughout the building.

Convinced that the former mill was haunted, CCTV cameras were installed and as the story spread some theories of the ghostly happenings came forward.

One story involved Helena Blundell, a young mill worker, who although she hated working here, had to remain to save up enough money to pursue her dream of being a singer. Just when she was ready to leave, she had an accident and fell down several stories to her death. This was on the same day as the Titanic hit the ice-burg in the Atlantic – April 14th, 1912. Poor Helena was doomed to spend eternity in the mill.

When a small fire started in the mill in 1999, a wax cylinder wrapped up in cloth was found in the building. Inside was an early recording of Helena singing – she had hid this away for safe keeping until her departure from the mill. This actual recording of Helena Blundell can be heard on You Tube.

The Ghosts of Pipe Lane Mill, Belfast

Pipe Lane Mill was one of the many mills operating in Belfast around the early 1900s.

A serious accident occurred in 1902 when part of the mill collapsed and heavy machinery in the upper floors crashed through to the lower levels. Many workers were injured and thirteen female mill workers were killed instantly. Within a year, the mill was up and working again. Since then, many ghostly sightings were seen over the years. One female ghost was seen at the top of a spiral staircase and then suddenly disappeared.

Another older lady was observed wandering around the machines in the spot where the accident had occurred. She was recognised by some of the workers as one of those who had been killed in the accident. When anyone approached her, she would instantly disappear.

Eventually, the building was vacated when the mill industry in Belfast declined.

Mussenden Temple Library, Co. Derry

Mussenden Temple is a small circular building, which is perched on a 120 feet cliff overlooking the Downhill Strand and the Atlantic Ocean near Castlerock. It was originally built as a library in imitation of an ancient Roman Temple in memory of the Bishop of Derry's cousin, Mrs. Frideswide Mussenden. The temple forms part of the Downhill Estate and is a tourist attraction and often used as a picturesque setting for weddings.

Mussenden Temple
(Courtesy of Phil Reiss)

It is said that a mysterious patch of blood sometimes appears on the floor of the Mussenden Temple and disappears a few minutes later.

Mussenden Temple overlooks Downhill Strand which was used for the windswept shore of Dragonstone in the Game Of Thrones series. Stannis Barathea launched his voyage to Blackwater Bay from here and Melisandra sacrificed statues of the seven gods of Westeros.

Molly The Friendly Ghost, Lisburn, Co. Antrim

This story begins in 1980 when a man, his wife and three children aged 9, 8 and 6 moved to a grand two storey four bed, terrace house in Llewellyn Avenue, on the Belfast Road, Lisburn. These houses were built in 1906 and had two bedrooms on the top floor, two in the middle floor and a bathroom and toilet to the rear along a long landing.

Downstairs consisted of a hallway, stairs, two good sized living rooms and a long dining / kitchen area to the rear. The family had only moved in about two weeks when some very strange, unexplained things started to happen. Their eight year-old daughter said she had seen an elderly lady on the first floor landing. She had a long dress on and was smiling. The young girl was not frightened at all.

A few days later, the family were rushing out of the house for an appointment. The children were in the car and the mother was just after changing into a skirt when she noticed the stitching along the side of the zipper was ripped. She took it off and put it over the banister stating, *"I'll repair that later"* and changed into another skirt. On their return later that evening she found the stitching along the zipper intact. Someone had fixed it while they were away.

The family had a little Yorkshire terrier dog at that time and in the evenings the dog was always downstairs. It is said that dogs have an instinct or senses for things unseen, so the father watched the dog's reaction when strange noises occurred inside the house. She pricked her ears up at the cubbyhole door under the stairs on several occasions. When the man opened the door she never would go in as if it was afraid to go any further. It also barked with a strange growl.

On another occasion, the father was decorating his bedroom and worked until late in the evening. He got washed, changed for bed and checked the children who were all fast asleep in their beds on the top floor. He turned off the light on the landing and went back into his bedroom. As he got into bed beside his wife he could see the reflection of the landing light coming on again in the mirror above the dressing table. It gave him a quite a fright because he knew it could not have been any of the children or his wife who had turned it on. The landing light remained on every night for the next three years even though it had been turned off.

On two different occasions as the parents were in bed, they both heard the noise of knives and forks being rattled in the kitchen. The couple's fourth child was a son, born in 1983 and he was only a few months old when the mother got the fright of her life. One morning about 11am, she was alone downstairs in the house when she heard what seemed like the loud noise of curtains being swished to and fro and coming from one of the bedrooms. The young child was asleep in that bedroom. A neighbour was called upon to assist and both went upstairs and found the child had slept through the noises. A voice could then he heard and it said, *"I am Molly and I'm not here to hurt you!"*

The strangest occurrence of all was on the night they were leaving to move to a new home in Banbridge. It was early December 1983 and almost all their belongings had been moved to the new house. It was dark and snowing and they had just placed the last few items in the car. One of the neighbours called to help with the final packing and as they were chatting about the strange happenings in the house, the water pipes suddenly started to rattle throughout the whole house for about five minutes. The noise continued as they pulled the front door closed behind them. A lady's voice could be heard saying, *"Goodbye, I will miss you!"*

None of the family was really frightened by the goings on in that house. Later, the man spoke to the new owners of the house and enquired if they had experienced anything strange but they had not.

In Bed With a Ghost, Belfast and Loughinisland, Co. Down

This was probably one of the most interesting stories we came across during our research. It was about a ghost that followed a family even when they moved house to a different part of the country. It all started in a house located in Stockman's Lane in Belfast. The occupants of the house had a small child and it would waken at the exact time every night as if it had a nightmare. The mother described how she could have timed to the very minute each night at 3am when the child would wake out of its sleep screaming with terror. It would take a half an hour or more to get it settled again. On another occasion the father was in the child's room and suddenly he noticed a figure standing at the door. He walked towards it and kicked out at the figure but there was nothing there. He turned on the light and it was gone. Then it felt as if a cloud of smoke had went into his mouth. The man found the whole experience very surreal and could not understand what it was.

The couple decided to leave the house and move to Loughinisland because they felt the house in Belfast had a presence, which may not have wanted them there. However, the ghost seemed to follow them because within a few weeks of moving, the strangest thing of all happened. One night the man was out for the night playing music and he was staying with a friend in Castlewellan. During the night his wife was lying in the bed and she felt a tug on the quilt. She thought it was her husband and said, *"I thought you said you weren't coming home tonight!"* She felt as if a full size body was lying beside her but there was no warmth coming from it. The woman turned around to see why she had not heard an answer and was shocked to see that there was no one there.

The couple was running out of options and as a last resort, decided to call on the services of a medium to visit their home and try to communicate with the spirit. The medium told them to imagine a gold or silver thread wrapping itself into a cocoon right in the centre of their eyes. Then they had to say the words, *"I don't need you here and I don't want you here!"* They had to repeat this phrase three times. After this, the couple never had any more encounters with the ghost. The medium was able to tell them that the ghost was the man's father who had died a few years previous and that he only wanted to make sure that they were all right. Strangely enough, after its departure, the woman found it quite lonely not having the spirit in the house because she was so used to its presence.

Ghost Forces Family to Emigrate, Rockacorry, Co. Monaghan

This story was reported in 1908 in the Londonderry Sentinel. A family living at Cormeen, near Rockacorry became so annoyed by the nightly visit of a woman dressed in a white robe. The latter would appear at the window, put her face close to the pane and peer into the house. She also apparently entered the dwelling and moved around inside, opening and closing the doors as if she owned the place. The family was forced to keep the lights on at night. After several years living here, the family decided to move far away.

Chapter 4

Workhouse Ghosts

From the 18th Century, workhouses were established throughout Ireland by Charitable Institutions to provide care for the poor. By 1838 an Act of Parliament extended the powers of the Poor Law Commissioners and plans were drawn for 130 new workhouses across the country. Examples were in Cootehill, Co. Cavan, Belfast and Lisburn Co. Antrim, Newry, Banbridge and Downpatrick in Co. Down. As the Great Famine developed, more and more people flocked to the workhouses. They became places of destitution and disease with many of the inmates dying. As one can imagine there are many sad and ghostly stories linked with the workhouses. Here is a selection: -

The Blue Guardian, Glendermott Road, Waterside, Co. Derry

The matron in charge of this old workhouse was very strict with anyone who infringed the rules. Children, as a form of punishment, would be locked away in an upstairs cupboard until they had learnt their lesson. No one could hear their cries!

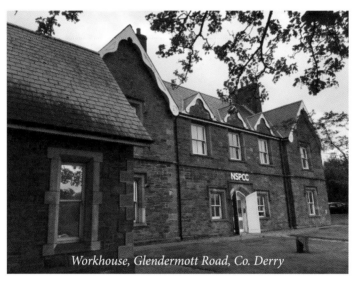

Workhouse, Glendermott Road, Co. Derry

The matron was suddenly called away as her sister was seriously ill. She left in such a hurry that she forgot that she had recently locked two small children in the cupboard. Only when her sister's health improved and she began to make plans to return to the workhouse, did the matron remember about them. She became frantic and could not wait to return to the workhouse but unfortunately her worst fears were confirmed and she found the remains of the children clinging to each other inside the locked cupboard. She screamed and was inconsolable until she finally gave up the will to live. Her lamenting ghost walks the corridors of the workhouse, which later became a hospital. Night nurses would catch fleeting glimpses of her and one such nurse, who was receiving treatment there, woke up during the night to see a woman dressed in white placing another blanket on her bed. She tucked the blanket in before disappearing through the wall of the room.

Downpatrick Workhouse, Co. Down

This workhouse was built in 1842 and consisted of a three-storey building. It housed many poor unfortunate people, young and old and many died there during the famine years. Hundreds of unknown paupers were buried in a field situated behind the workhouse. The former workhouse has long since been demolished but prior to that it was used for a time as a leather factory after the Second World War.

Downpatrick Workhouse

Many of the workers in the leather factory would experience strange happenings, unexplained noises and changes in temperature. One day a worker was in the store when he felt a chill and a tingling of the hairs on the back of his neck. He turned round and noticed a small old man wearing an old-fashioned flat cap walk across the room and suddenly disappear at one of the windows. The workman was so frightened that he rushed from the store and refused to go back inside unless someone else came with him. The following day, news came to the factory that a former workhouse employee had died and his description fitted that of the ghostly figure seen in the storeroom.

Once during the night shift, workers heard noises coming from the second floor of the factory. Thinking it was burglars they rushed upstairs. They observed a door at the end of one of the corridors lying open but there was no one about. Just then another door opened at the opposite end of the same corridor and a door in the middle also opened. The men searched the whole area but could find no one. Eventually, they believed that the only explanation for the strange happening was that the ghosts of the workhouse were causing the doors to open.

Another story relating to the workhouse involves a local lady who once observed a little girl dressed in Victorian clothes and standing close by the old workhouse building. Thinking she needed help to cross the road, the lady stopped her car but as she got out and looked back, the little girl had disappeared.

Tramps Terrified at Clones Workhouse, Co. Cavan

The following story was reported in the Irish Independent Newspaper in May 1905. The name Clones is from 'Cluain Eois' meaning 'Eos's meadow' or 'Cluan Inis' meaning 'island of retreat' as it was once surrounded by water.

One night, two tramps were sleeping in one of the wards of the former workhouse when they were awakened by a noise and saw an apparition climbing up the stairs into the ward. They described the figure as tall and terrible as they could see it by the light of the moon. It approached the men and pulled the beds from under them and tossed the clothes away. They screamed so loud that the night porter wakened and ran to the ward unlocking the door. The two men ran out, almost naked and one of them immediately fainted.

Under no circumstances would the men return to the ward and begged the porter to let them stay near him for the rest of the night. Nothing would induce them to once again face the supernatural perils of the night before and they left early the following morning vowing to give Clones a wide berth in the future.

Clones Workhouse, Co. Cavan

The night porter was convinced the men had definitely seen something as he had seen the terrified look in their eyes.

The same ghostly vision was reported some months later when a man named Johnston, from Ballybay, Co. Cavan saw the form of a man cross the ward floor and open up one of the folded down beds and then lie down. Mr. Johnston managed to get back to sleep but the next morning there was no-one there and when he enquired about the visitor the next morning, he was informed that there were no other admissions during the night.

Banbridge Workhouse, Co. Down

There have been numerous sightings of ghosts walking around the grounds of the workhouse and on the road near the site of the former which now houses the new Health Centre and Polyclinic. These sightings have included a man walking in the grounds near the perimeter fence who then suddenly disappears. On a separate occasion, two people crossed the road in front of another local person one night beside the old hospital and they also suddenly vanished. Local people claim that these are the spirits of the deceased former inmates of the workhouse or of former patients from the hospital, which was built on the same site.

An artist's impression of Banbridge Workhouse (J.Spence)

When workmen were digging out the foundations for the new Health Clinic, they discovered some human bones. The area may have been used as the burial ground for some of the deceased inmates from the workhouse.

The Union Workhouse, Lisburn Road, Belfast

This workhouse is now the site of the old City Hospital in Belfast and is said to have been haunted. Once there was a cruel warden working here. He was known to have locked up inmates in the Lunatic Asylum Section and beat them until they would die. One such male inmate was chained to the cell floor and later died there. Afterwards, there was an inquest but no explanation could be given as to why the body was covered in bruises. Apparently, a strange figure dressed in ragged clothes was often seen haunting the workhouse any time a suspicious death in the asylum occurred. Eventually, the rules of the workhouse were amended and no more suspicious deaths happened at the hands of the warden.

The Roe Valley Hospital, Limavady, Co. Derry

The Roe Valley Hospital was a former workhouse dating from the mid 1800s. It then became a hospital in 1936 and is now used as an administrative building.

Former Workhouse in Limavady, Co. Derry

Stories exist where people have heard the sound of crying babies and others have seen ghostly figures of men and women in uniform. Once a security officer caught a ghostly image on his camera – it resembled a woman holding a baby wearing an old-fashioned bonnet and clothing. By all accounts the photograph appears to be authentic.

The lost souls of those inmates who died here are said to still haunt the building. Some gruesome stories exist from the old hospital including that of a pregnant nurse. She hid her pregnancy as she was unmarried and delivered the baby herself. She then killed it and became very remorseful and unable to live with herself afterwards. She ended up taking her own life at the hospital.

Some people claimed to have seen a nurse in an old-fashioned cape and a red hood waiting by the bridge at the front of the hospital. And when it operated as a hospital the night staff would hear the sound of a former nurse who had a wooden leg limping around the wards in the early hours.

The bridge in front of the former workhouse

Chapter 5

Ghostly Tales of Churches & Places of Worship

Bonamargy Abbey, Ballycastle, Co. Antrim

The ruins of Bonamargy Friary lie between the beach and Ballycastle on the North Antrim Coast. The name Bonamargy comes from 'Bun na Margaí' meaning 'foot of the River Margy'.

The Friary was originally founded in 1500 by the Franciscans and after it was damaged by Elizabeth I's troops around 1584, it was rebuilt by the MacDonnell Clan.

'The Black Nun', Julia MacQuillan was a 17th Century prophet and recluse and her dying wish was to be buried at the entrance to the chapel so that she would be walked over by those entering the little chapel. Her grave is marked by a worn Celtic Cross at the west end of the chapel. The Black Nun lived alone here in her cell until 1641 when the friary stopped being used. It is said that she was murdered on the steps leading up to the upper floor falling on the thirteenth step. Legend states that bad luck will befall anyone who walks on it! Julia had a sister who came to her to seek forgiveness for her sins. At first, Julia refused to give her sister absolution and later when she changed her mind, she emerged to find the dead body of her sister in the grounds of the chapel.

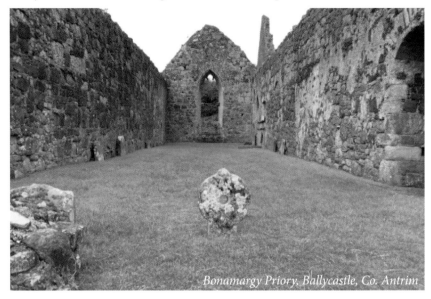

Bonamargy Priory, Ballycastle, Co. Antrim

It is said that Julia regretted her decision and her sorrowful ghost now haunts the ruins. There have been sightings of a ghostly dark-robed nun while others have seen strange lights around the church.

Another legend is that if you walk around her grave seven times in a clockwise direction and then seven times anti-clockwise and put your hand through the hole in her tombstone, you will be able to summon up her ghost.

The Black Nun was also known as a prophet, for example, that the time would come that there would be no difference between summer and winter except for the leaves of the trees, also that ships would be made from iron and that there would be horse-less carriages.

Grey Abbey, Co. Down

Grey Abbey is a ruined Cistercian monastery situated on the shores of Strangford Lough. It dates from the 12th Century and was founded by the Norman, John de Courcy's wife, Affreca. It was then burnt by Brian O'Neill and later refurbished by Sir Hugh Montgomery, one of the Ulster Planters.

Grey Abbey, Co. Down

A number of ghosts are said to haunt the ruins. One is a young man, dressed in period clothes, who appears to be carrying a package and who suddenly disappears beneath one of the arches. The other ghosts include three ladies dressed in Victorian attire with their parasols who seem to float along the ruins and then fade away. The ghosts do not appear to be concerned about anyone being there and just carry on in their parallel world.

Ghosts of the Old Drumballyroney Church, Co. Down

Just south of Rathfriland on the Banbridge Road lies the old Drumballyroney Church and adjoining Bronte School.

Hundreds of years ago the church used to be a Catholic Chapel and was close to the seat of the Magennis Clan who used to worship there and where some were buried. The church itself would have dated from the 14th century but it was destroyed by Cromwellian Forces in the 17th century. A replacement church was later built on the site and it still stands today. However, it is claimed that it is built over the Magennis's graves and the former memorial stone was broken up and thrown into a ditch.

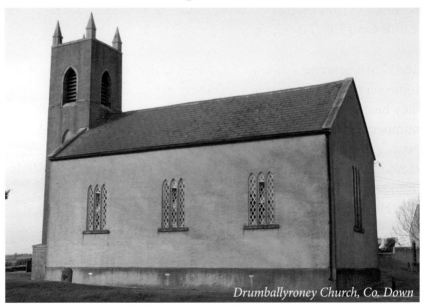

Drumballyroney Church, Co. Down

People also claim that on the anniversary of the death of the Chief Magennis, a noise can be heard inside the church coming from beneath the floor. It sounds as if someone is trying to get out. In the 1800s, a local minister heard the knocking sound and thought perhaps it was an animal trapped under the floor. He prised open some of the floorboards to investigate and it is said that the ghost of Magennis suddenly appeared in front of him.

He was so frightened that he ran home. However, when he had calmed down, the next day, he brought two men with him to help him find out more. They searched further and discovered skulls and other human bones beneath the floor. They then sealed the floor. The same minister who used to have black hair turned very white shortly afterwards. Meanwhile the distant knocking can still be heard!

Both the church and the school are said to be haunted by the Bronte family. Patrick Bronte, the father of the famous Bronte novelists, was at one time the minister and he also taught in the school. His spirit is said to roam the church and the adjacent graveyard at night. Another spirit was Squire Hawkins who is buried in the adjacent graveyard. He was a member of the Rathfriland Hell Fire Club.

The Ghost Searchers Ireland Team visited the church and made some very interesting findings. During their investigation, they heard footsteps walking up the aisle of the Church and a number of them saw a figure walking around the graveyard. A photographer also took some photos inside the church and there seemed to be strange light anomalies in the photographs. While inside the school the investigators recording equipment picked up a child saying that her name was Molly and that she attended the school. The ghost also stated that there were six pupils at the school. It did not seem that the ghost was annoyed with the investigators for being there but rather that she wanted to communicate with them.

Another person made contact with the investigators. He said the words *"Bronte School"* and added that his name was Patrick. Could this be the ghost of Patrick Bronte? During the recording you can clearly hear these words being spoken. Throughout the night the whole team were extremely cold and they could feel a presence.

Whilst in the church something or someone tried to take the camera off the cameraman and their recording device was knocked over. On the video you can see a wire on the woman's headphones being tugged. The investigators also heard a large bang and footsteps and a few knocks towards the back of the church. Their camera went strangely out of focus and eventually they had to stop recording. Many of them believed that it might have been the infamous Squire Hawkins letting his presence be known. (See Chapter 6)

Dunlewy Church, Co. Donegal

The name Dunlewy is derived from 'Dún Lúiche' which means 'fort of Lugh', an ancient Irish God.

Dunlewy Church, Co. Donegal

The old ruined church at Dunlewy stands solitary at the foot of Mount Errigal overlooking the 'Poisoned Glen' and has all the appearance of a mysterious place. It was built in the mid 19th Century from locally quarried white marble. The legend of the Poisoned Glen comes from the story of Lugh who slew Balor. Poison then escaped from Balor's eye over the whole glen.

Poisoned Glen Sign, Dunlewy, Co. Donegal

As the Dunlewy Estate declined, the church fell into ruins. Few people will go near the old Church of Dunlewy believing it to be haunted.

The Mystery Of The Great Bell Of Inch Abbey, Co. Down

Inch Abbey is a late 12th century Cistercian Abbey situated on the banks of the Quoile River, near Downpatrick.

A great bell once hung in the Abbey and was used by the monks to warn the simple village people nearby of death and destruction as rampaging Vikings swept across County Down. However, the Abbey itself was later destroyed and its bell disappeared. It is said that the monks took it out on the river and let it sink to be buried in the deep river mud to prevent its capture. The traditional poem 'The Burial of the Bell' tells how the monks rowed away from the Abbey and when they plunged the mighty bell into the water, they recited these words, *"No hand shall desecrate it, no tyrant stamp it slave"*.

Inch Abbey, Co. Down

The bell has never been found despite many searches of the river. It is said that the bell still sounds occasional warnings from its watery grave.

When Co. Down is threatened by invaders or if some evil force descends on the area, it is rumoured that the Great Bell of Inch will peal again as a warning to its population.

A local lady used to regularly see a boat with three men in it out on the Quoile River. Two of the men were rowing and the third was working with a rope at the stern. When she mentioned this to her husband who had been with her at all of these so-called sightings, he admitted that he had never seen the boat and neither had anyone else. The lady who had psychic powers, remembered that the men appeared to be wearing brown sweaters but now believes that she had witnessed the spirits of the Abbey monks, dressed in their brown habits as they buried the Great Bell.

Chapter 6
Ghosts & Transport

Ghosts are not just confined to stately homes and castles. There are many tales related to trains, roads, cars, horse and carriages and boats. One story exists of a ghostly ship, which is said to forewarn those who see it of an impending disaster. The 'Flying Dutchman' is probably the most famous of such ghost or phantom ships. Its legend tells of a ship sailing around the Cape of Good Hope during a very bad storm. The captain would not let the crew take the ship in to one of the safe harbours in the area as he insisted the ship would be safe and not sink. As the crew prayed for their safety, a glowing form appeared on the deck of the ship and the crew believed it was the image of Christ. The captain however dismissed the apparition and boasted that even God could not sink his ship! The spirit then placed a curse on the ship and doomed it to sail the seas forever and to bring bad luck to any sailor who might see it.

Nearly all the older railway stations are favourite places for ghostly sightings. Belfast's York Road Station is listed in the top ten most haunted railway stations in the United Kingdom

York Road Old Train Station, Belfast

The original station was built in 1848 by the former Belfast & Ballymena Railway and lasted until 1992 when services were transferred to other railway stations in Belfast.

During the 1970s, one of its workmen was killed during a bungled robbery and over the years there has been reports of a ghostly figure in and around the station. Commuters would have seen such a figure sitting in the locked canteen at night and then it would suddenly disappear.

A ghostly figure was also seen around the station's running sheds. At night strange footsteps could be heard in the station even though no one else was there. Was this the ghost of the worker whose life came to an abrupt end all those years ago?

Strabane Railway Station Ghost, Co. Tyrone

Another strange story has emerged from Strabane Railway Station in the 1950s. One night, four railway workers were working in one of the engine sheds when they heard a terrible commotion coming from another shed. The sound of wailing, crying and loud bangs caused the workers to rush over to investigate. In the darkness they witnessed a dark shadowy figure staring out at them with a menacing glare. They left the shed and even though they were shaking, tried to continue with their work while the banging and wailing continued. When the noise eventually stopped, they plucked up the courage to go inside the other shed again. Stepping inside, there was nothing there. Where had the mystery figure gone?

The following night, the same thing happened again and the ghostly figure appeared to three of the railway workers. After that night, it was never seen again but their story remains a mystery to this day.

The South Armagh Ghost Train, Co. Armagh

The main Belfast to Dublin train passes through County Down and Armagh before it crosses the border after it leaves Killeen. Sightings of a strange train began at the early part of this century. One such sighting was by a railway official who lived close to the railway and whose job was to attend one of the gates. As all scheduled trains had passed for the night he was very surprised to hear a train approaching from the North. As it was his duty to be present at the gates with his lamp, he went outside and observed the passenger train emerging from 'The Wellington Cutting' in Killeen but when it travelled on to a place called 'Barney's Bridge' it suddenly disappeared! He walked to bridge but could see nothing.

The next day, the railway man relayed his story and other people also admitted that they also had heard the ghost train and it stopping at Barney's Bridge. The railway man's cottage became the centre of attention and many people gathered there at night to wait for the train to pass again. Their patience was eventually rewarded and one night after all the scheduled trains had gone, another train was heard approaching. The gateman went outside with his lamp while others remained inside and looked out of the window. Everyone was amazed to see the lighted carriages of the train emerging from the cutting and then disappear at the bridge.

Those who believe in ghosts maintain that most sightings are connected with a tragic event that occurred in that particular place. In this area, the most tragic railway disaster ever to occur in Ireland took place a short distance from where the sightings were reported.

One June morning in 1889, a busy train set out from Armagh to Warrenpoint. The passengers included children who were on their annual excursion with the Methodist Church. It is estimated that there were up to twelve hundred people on board. The train struggled to climb the hill and it stopped, as the engine was unable to deal with the heavy load. It was decided to split the train in two, bringing one half of the carriages over the hill and then coming back for the other ones. Stones were placed under the wheels of the back carriages to prevent them rolling backwards.

When the engine once again started, it suddenly jerked backwards and crashed into the back carriages. The stones underneath the wheels were crushed and the back carriages started to move backwards down the hill picking up speed as they descended. Some passengers managed to jump clear but many of the doors were locked, as there were so many children on board. Those on board were terrified especially so when they observed another train coming.

There was a massive collision. Many carriages were smashed to pieces and the engine of the oncoming train was thrown aside like a little toy. Meanwhile, the front end of the first train was also rolling back when one of the railway men managed to apply the hand brakes. He was badly injured in the process and died later. Many men, women and children were killed and badly injured as a result of the crash. Dead bodies littered the embankment and the injured were heard screaming from inside the trains. The disaster sent shock waves throughout the country and the final death toll was eighty-eight.

Many argue that the sighting of the ghost train is connected with this disaster as they occurred in the same area, however, other rail tragedies have happened in the area. One such tragedy was in 1921 when three special trains were coming back from Belfast to the Curragh after the official opening of the N. I. Parliament by King George V. The third train was blown up killing three soldiers and a guard as well as forty horses, used by the 10th Hussars. All the horses were buried nearby.

The sighting of the 'ghost train' is believed to be a warning of a pending railway crash. Even during the 'Troubles' it re-appeared just before a train carrying troops was blown up 'within a mile of Adavoyle', according to a local ballad. Adavoyle is situated about a mile from where the ghost train is said to disappear.

The Railway Ghost of Ballymacarrett, Belfast

Ballymacarrett comes from 'Baile Mhic Gearóid' meaning MacCarrett's townland' and is a suburb of Belfast in the parish of Knockbreda.

It was a cold dark night at the end of the 20th Century when a railway signal man was coming off duty on the Co. Down railway. He was walking through dense fog on the railway track, which ran above the winding streets of East Belfast.

The 7.30pm Bangor train had just passed him when he heard footsteps behind him. Eventually, he was able to make out the figure of a woman approaching him through the fog. The two of them walked and talked along the railway as far as the station where he bade the woman goodnight. After signing off work, he made his way to a local public house and met up with some of his fellow workmates.

The Railway Train, Ballymacarrett Belfast

In the pub, he recounted his meeting with his work colleagues. One of them was startled to hear him say that the woman's name was Hanvey. He explained that there had been a very bad incident in 1896 when a local man stumbled across the body of a young woman along the railway. The body was later identified as Catherine Hanvey, a single woman, aged thirty, who worked as a domestic servant in a house on the Lisburn Road in Belfast. At her inquest, it was concluded that she had been killed by a train.

The railway signalman could not believe his ears when he heard the story. It was obvious that he woman had returned to haunt the railway.

Road Ghost Stories

Stories of vanishing travellers have occurred throughout the centuries and while the types of vehicles have changed, the basic sequence of events has remained the same.

The Ghost of Barnesmore Gap, Co. Donegal

Barnesmore Gap is a mountain pass located in the Bluestack Mountains of Donegal. Its name in Irish is 'An Bearnas Mór' and means the 'big gap'.

This story appeared on the Donegal Daily and was told by a well-respected local man. One winter's night in 1983, he was driving to Donegal Town from Ballybofey where he had been at a dance in a local hotel. It was around 2.30am and as he climbed through the Barnesmore Gap, he had to keep the wipers on to see out of the sleet. He also lost reception of his favourite RTE radio channel and had to switch to another.

He remarked that he did not meet any other vehicles on this stretch, which was unusual even at such a late time but just as he approached the Castlederg turn-off he saw a young woman standing at the side of the road waving her arm. He had drove past her before he was able to stop and before he reversed back to give her a lift, the rear door of the car opened and she climbed inside. He was puzzled how fast she had moved to reach his car so quickly. He asked her to let him know where she wanted left off and she answered, *"Yes"* but it sounded more like a hiss. The driver was feeling a bit uneasy with this passenger and kept glimpsing back at her in his rear-view mirror as he drove through the darkness.

Although she was very close to the side window, her breath did not cause any steam on it. The temperature in the car suddenly dropped even though the heater was switched on full. They passed by Biddy's Pub and about another mile up the road; she whispered, *"Stop here"*. She then whispered again, *"Stop here...this is where I died"*.

Slamming on the brakes, the driver looked behind but the seat was empty but the car door was still closed. Suddenly, the RTE Radio channel started playing again as the 3.00am news was announced. The driver was perplexed as to what had happened and never understood that strange event.

The Phantom Car of Barnesmore Gap, Co. Donegal

Another strange story has emerged from the Barnesmore Gap. In the 1930s, the Derry Journal reported how many people were visiting the road to try to catch sight of a phantom motorcar which has been seen regularly every night over the past few months. It was said to travel at great speed with its full headlights on and just within yards of the observer, it suddenly disappears!

The newspaper actually interviewed some of the witnesses of this strange occurrence. One man actually pulled his horse and cart to the side of the road to allow the car to pass by. Another lady claimed to have seen the head and face of the male driver before it disappeared. Several theories were put forward to explain the

sudden appearance and disappearance of the car but many still
believe that this was indeed a ghostly phenomenon.

The Girl from Ballymullan, Co. Down

Most ghost stories concerning children are centred on a tragic
event and the following is no exception. People also believe that
animals, particularly horses see things, which are not visible to
the human eye. There are many stories about horses that refuse to
pass a certain place or become so frightened that they bolt and run
away. Some say that if you looked into the horse's eyes at that time,
one will see a reflection of what it actually saw.

Ballymullan is a small townland lying between Crawfordsburn
and Helen's Bay in County Down. Its name is drawn from 'Baile Uí
Mhaoláin' meaning 'Mullan's townland'. In the late 1920s, a man
was driving his horse and cart along the road when he noticed
a young and very pale girl standing at the side of the road. His
horse became very unsettled as they passed the girl, however, she
herself paid no attention to the horse and cart and appeared to
stare right through them. Curious, the man stopped to ask if the
girl was alright but when he looked back, she had disappeared. He
dismounted and searched all around but to no avail and then his
horse suddenly bolted and galloped along the road. Eventually, he
caught up with the horse and saw that it was very distressed. He
walked alongside it for some distance to calm it down.

Reaching a small cottage he asked for some water for the horse
and then told the occupants the story of the little girl. Immediately,
they were able to tell him of a tragedy that occurred along that
particular stretch of road. Years previously, a young girl had fallen
from a lorry and had been killed. Other people had also told of
seeing her ghost standing at the roadside.

Strange Happenings at Ballyjamesduff, Co Cavan

In the 1930s, a new drainage scheme was started near the town of Ballyjamesduff. For safety reasons, the contractor erected a watchman's hut so that the works could be guarded at night.

One of the first watchmen was an ex-soldier. While inside the hut, at midnight, he started to feel very uncomfortable as if he was not alone. He became very frightened and quickly left the hut and went home. A new watchman was employed for the following night. Unfortunately, he only lasted one night and resigned the following morning stating that he had seen the ghost of a woman. The story spread throughout the district and by the third night, over two hundred people had gathered to accompany the new night watchman. However, nothing unusual happened.

It was recalled that over twenty-two years previously, an old woman was returning from Ballyjamesduff on a wet and stormy night. She fell into a deep drain and was drowned. Many believed that the new drainage works had disturbed her spirit!

Roadside Ghost, Upper Lough Erne, Co. Fermanagh

This story was told by Hugh Nolan in 'Passing the Time' by Henry Glassie.

Just after WWII, a group of friends were passing a viaduct when they noticed there had been a motorcar accident. They helped out and gave the driver a lift home, which was down a country lane. Suddenly, a man stepped out in front of the car and in the glare of the headlights, they recognised a man who they all knew had recently died. No matter what way the driver turned the wheels to avoid the man on the road; he remained in front of the car. It was only when they reached a crossroads that the driver was able to make a sharp turn and escape.

Hugh was a brother of one of the occupants in the car and to this day no one is able to explain what happened.

A1 Ghost Stories, Co. Down

The A1 is a major road that runs through County Down and mainly from Newry to Belfast. Over forty years ago, a local man was driving along a stretch of the A1 in the early hours of the morning. The road would have been a single carriageway at that time. Coming round a bend, he noticed a young man standing at the side of the road. He appeared to be soldier as he was wearing a heavy coat and had a kit bag over his shoulder and looked as if he was waiting for a lift. After passing the soldier, the curious driver looked back in his mirror but there was no sign of the soldier. He stopped his car and looked all around for the soldier but no one was there. What had the driver seen? Was this soldier a vision from the past?

Another story from the A1 involves another driver coming home from his work in Belfast one dark winter's evening. Suddenly, he saw a young woman in her early twenties looking for a lift. He noticed that although she wore a coat, she did not have any bag or gloves. Concerned about her well-being and being a father himself, he stopped to give the woman a lift. Not a word was spoken by her even when the driver asked where she was going. Some distance on, the driver felt an icy chill and he turned to look at his passenger only to discover that she had vanished!

He was so startled that he slammed on his brakes and then managed to stumble outside. But there was no one there! He even checked the passenger door but was satisfied that there was no way that the woman could have got out of his car without him noticing. Eventually, he calmed down and managed to drive further and he went to the nearest police station where he reported his tale of the Phantom Hitch Hiker.

Another similar story involves the Comber to Newtownards Dual Carriageway. A driver noticed a blonde haired girl standing at the side of this main road. As this was somewhat unusual along such a busy dual carriageway, the driver looked back at her in his mirror but there was no sign of her. He pulled in and got out of the car for a closer look and could not see her anywhere. He was very puzzled as there was no clear exit off the road at this particular spot.

Ghost seen in Glencolmcille, Co. Donegal

Glencolmcille is situated in the Gaeltacht Region of S.W. Donegal. The following story was reported in the Newsletter in 1939 and involved the appearance of a ghost at the Yellow Brae between Gannew and Dunroe.

Two young men were walking on this road late one night when they suddenly saw a very strange tall figure dressed in a while coat. It crossed the road in front of them and disappeared in to a briar bush at the side of the road. The men were curious and investigated further but when they looked beyond the bus, all they could see were two long legs gliding off in the distance but none of the body was visible.

The same figure was seen by an elderly woman who collapsed at the scene. The ghost was said to be that of a local wealthy yeoman's son who died tragically at this spot near the end of the 18th Century.

The Snow Storm, Co. Cavan

In the late 1950s, a man named Tom Dolan had returned home to a very remote part of Co. Cavan with his young family after living many years in England. Tom was determined to raise his family in his native homeland away from the intensity of a large city and was quite prepared to endure any hardships put in his way.

However, during his first winter back home, one of the worst snowstorms in living memory struck the county and by the evening of the second day, his wife became worried about food running low. Tom took it upon himself to make the long trek to the local village to secure whatever he could get and carry back home.

All that was available was a sack of flour, which he gratefully accepted knowing his wife was a good baker and would be able to keep the family fed. Sacks of flour in those days were not like the handy little bags we can now purchase in supermarkets. Tom's bag weighed nearly a cwt. and it had to be carried on his back through the deepening snow.

As Tom made his way home again, the wind picked up making it virtually impossible for him to see through the blizzard conditions. He soon became disorientated and worried that he would not even reach home alive. He thought of his wife and children and how they would survive without him. At his worst moment, when he was knee deep in snow and struggling with the large bag of flour, something strange happened.

Just in front of him, a tall figure dressed in black appeared. Tom did not recognise the man and wondered that he appeared not be to affected by the snow. The figure kept pointing at the footprints he was leaving behind in the snow and for Tom to follow the same tracks. Tom gratefully followed the path and soon they were both at his cottage and home safely. When Tom turned around to thank the tall stranger and invite him in, he was nowhere to be seen!

Some days later, when the snow storm had died down, Tom could not wait to relay his story to everyone he met in the hope that he could find out the identity of the strange man who had saved him in the storm. Unfortunately, no one could help except for an old postman who had heard stories many years ago of the same ghostly figures who had led people to safety in the same way.

City of Derry Airport, Co. Derry

The following is an unusual story concerning Derry City Airport. Situated near Eglinton village on the outskirts of Derry, the airport was used by the RAF during WWII and then later as a base for Eglinton Flying Club. Since the late 1980s, it has been run by Derry City Council with airlines such as Ryanair and BMI operating from it.

Derry City Airport, Co. Derry

Over the years many men had lost their lives when landing their planes or when taking off. A former employee in the airport tells of how when she was working in the kitchen, she suddenly felt very cold and a rather unpleasant smell came from behind her. When she turned around, she saw a man dressed in a WWII uniform standing beside one of the fridges. He looked sad and tired and while she stared at the figure, he suddenly disappeared. Another member of staff entered the kitchen quickly afterwards and commented on how cold it was.

Although she had heard stories before where staff had seen men in war uniforms walking around the grass slipways near the runway and then disappearing, this was the first occasion that she, herself, had seen anything strange.

Warrenpoint's Ghost Ship, Co. Down

The seaside town of Warrenpoint lies on the Co. Down side of Carlingford Lough. It has its own 'phantom ship' – 'The Lord Blaney'. It appears as an old-fashioned steam packet and it is said that it sails up to the pier in Warrenpoint and then disappears.

In 1833, the Lord Blaney made its final journey across the Irish Sea to Liverpool. It was packed with passengers, livestock and other cargo. Despite an overnight sailing in very rough conditions, the ship reached the entrance to the Merseyside estuary. However, in the mist, it hit a sandbank and very quickly the ship broke in two parts. The passengers, crew and animals all fell into the sea and were swept away. Only one living creature reached the shore and that was the famous Irish racehorse 'Monteagle'.

On several occasions, the ghostly image of the ship has been seen in Warrenpoint Harbour and after each appearance; a local ship has been lost at sea. One such tragedy occurred in 1916 when the passenger ship the 'SS Connemara', which sailed between Greenore and Holyhead, collided with a coal boat the 'SS Retriever'. The ferry sank with the loss of ninety-seven lives. It was reported that the Lord Blaney had been seen before the tragedy!

Ghostly Sightings on Carlingford Lough

The strangest of true stories can be absolutely terrifying for those who bear witness to them. Such was the case of two fishermen in an old wooden rowing boat on Carlingford Lough between Counties Down and Louth just south of Greencastle and Greenore in the spring of 1905.

Just as they did every day for over twenty two years, they rowed out to their favourite fishing ground which experience had taught them provided the best chance of landing the shoals of herring that was their living. The day began like any other but the longed for hope of a prize catch did not materialise and as dusk approached they decided to make their way home with only a meagre catch.

They were suddenly alerted to thundering, beating noises in the water some way behind their boat. They soon picked out the astonishing sight of about twenty frightened horses swimming for their lives towards them. Shouting and yelling in panic, the men tried to scare the horses away from their boat. They feared that they were going to be swamped. However, it was no use and soon the petrified animals were almost on top of them.

They both lay down flat in the bottom of their boat amid the few fish they had caught and watched as the spectre of the ghostly animals seemingly passed straight through their boat and then literally disappeared. When the fishermen emerged to look around in the fading light, there was nothing to see or hear.

Back on land, they decided nervously to ask around if anyone had ever experienced the same strange event, which had, befell them. However, no one had ever heard of such a sighting and as they feared, the fishermen began to become the butt of many jokes. They were often asked what part they had played in the 'Aquatic Grand National'.

The view of Carlingford Lough from the Flagstaff

A few months passed and the County Down men were once again out herring fishing. They noticed a storm brewing and decided to shelter in a little bay not far from King John's Castle in Carlingford. They decided to pass away a few hours in a local hostelry while the storm passed. They fell into the company of an old man and related their strange story to him.

He did not seem at all surprised and shaking his head, he told them it had been a very long time since anyone had reported the sighting of the unfortunate horses. The men were relieved that at long last someone believed their story and could now offer them an explanation.

The legendary story dates back hundreds of years to when a ship carrying horses to the then garrison town of Carlingford had been caught up in a ferocious storm. The crew decided to save themselves and the ship by forcefully dumping the unfortunate and terrified animals over the side. Even above the noise of the storm, the poor horses could be heard neighing and screaming in terror as they attempted to swim for their lives.

For many years after the terrible ordeal, the horses were often seen in all weathers and always in twilight still terrified and fighting for their lives somewhere out on Carlingford Lough between the coasts of County Down and County Louth.

Another ghostly tale has emerged from Carlingford Lough and involved two Scottish cyclists who were on a camping holiday. They had set up camp on a quiet river delta a few yards from the shore and as it was late and fairly dark, they concentrated on erecting their tent and cooking their evening meal. They never got a chance to study their surroundings and tired from the long day in the saddle, they quickly fell asleep.

At around 3 am, they were awakened by something and peering nervously out of their tent, an astonishing sight met their eyes.

Docked on the riverbank was an ancient three-masted sailing ship of the type used on long sea voyages many years ago. The gangplank was lowered and they could see human figures embarking, some carrying bags or cases while others seemed to have belongings wrapped up in little cloth bundles.

This carried on for more than fifteen minutes until a dark cloud obscured the moon and everything turned into darkness. The cyclists retreated back into their tent knowing daybreak was only a couple of hours away and they would then try and wish bon voyage to some of those on board the ship.

However, a thick fog had descended over the land and sea the next morning and they would have to wait a little longer to make their acquaintance with the ship and its passengers. But as the fog lifted, the ship was nowhere to be seen and closer investigation showed that in fact no ship could ever have possibly negotiated into what remained of a very old and rotten wooden wharf. The inlet was completely silted up and so badly that it was doubtful if even a rowing boat could have navigated its way in.

All the cyclists could do was to pack up their tent and move on hoping to meet someone locally who might be able to throw some light on their experience the night before. They did not have to wait long as they came across and old farmer who was using real horsepower to plough one of his fields. The pair excitedly approached him and told him their story. But he really surprised them by telling them to, *"Stop your story right there!"* The farmer then related what had happened as if he had been there himself. He continued, *"I have often heard old folk talk about this phenomenon but I never seen it myself"*.

Apparently, the legend states that one hundred and fifty years or so before, a bad illness or as we would describe now as an epidemic had ravished the entire area. Many old people were unable to withstand it and died. The younger people were now left homeless, as the landlords had repossessed the houses previously tenanted by the older folk. They were forced to sell whatever they had to try and get the few pennies needed to move away from the area.

A rather cantankerous sea captain appeared on the scene and offered passage on his ship for the 'right money'. He insisted on as many people as possible be carried as of course the more paying passengers, the more money he pocketed.

The legend also describes bad fogs around that time and the ship was believed to have left at night and possibly in one of the fogs. Whatever the truth was, the ship and its passengers were never heard from again. Did the captain return in spirit with his ship in the hope of finally getting his passengers to their destination? No one really knows!

The Ferryboat Ghost, Portaferry, Co. Down

In 1836, the 'Lady of the Lake' was the name given to the first steam-powered ferryboat, which operated across Strangford Lough between Portaferry and Strangford. Among her first passengers was a newly married couple who were setting off on their honeymoon.

In 1838, one very stormy October evening, the lough itself was extremely rough but the ferry made its journey across. The stormy sea tossed the ferry and its passengers decided to shelter in the passenger cabin. One of these making the crossing to Portaferry was called McHenry and unfortunately he was the worse for drink. There were two doors leading off the deck, one to the cabin and the other to the gearing and the paddle wheel. As the boat pitched and rolled in the tide, poor McHenry lost his balance and as he slipped on the wet deck, he was flung headfirst into the gearing for the paddlewheel and was instantly killed.

His body was eventually brought ashore and taken into one of the nearby cottages. Someone went to inform his family but as it was such a bad night, his family did not arrive until the next morning to take his body home.

Some years later, a sailor and his wife occupied the cottage where McHenry's body had been taken. The sailor was often away and his wife was left on her own for long periods of time. On another wet and windy night, one of the sailor's friends knocked at the cottage door and asked for shelter for himself and his donkey. A bed was made up for the man in the downstairs room and the donkey was sheltered in the yard at the back of the cottage. The next morning, she asked her visitor if he had slept well. He replied that he had endured a dreadful night.

Somewhat surprised, the woman asked why. She was told that although the bed was very comfortable and the room was warm, he had been wakened by the noise of someone at the bottom of the stairs. The visitor managed to sit up and light a candle and then saw the ghost of a man so severely mutilated and covered in blood that he was unable to identify him at first. The ghost was trying to climb the stairs but appeared to be very drunk and kept falling back and cursing as he did so. When he called out sharply from his bed, the bloody ghost disappeared. Immediately, the sailor's wife who had never heard the story of McHenry and had never witnessed any ghostly sightings, left the cottage. She ran to the local priest and insisted that her home be blessed and rid of this spectre forever.

Chapter 7
Ghostly Tales about Animals

The Gray Man's Path, Ballycastle, Co. Antrim

Just outside Ballycastle on the North Antrim coast is the headland known as Fair Head. This is indeed a mythical place with an ancient passage grave nearby. There is a lough in the centre of Fair Head containing a crannog – an artificial island built some thousands of years ago and used as a safe place to live and for livestock. Another small lough near the top of the headland known as the Black Lough or 'Lough Dhu' has the reputation of being haunted.

Underneath its waters lies the ghost of a devil-horse and when the mists come down it rears its head out of the water and takes the form of an old gray man. This ghostly figure wanders around the area in the bad light, trying to lure unsuspecting travellers to the lake edge and then drags them into the water. The area is know as the Gray Man's Path and at one point it continues along a fallen rock that has been jammed between two cliffs where it sits precariously above the steep crevice.

Gray Man's Path, Ballyclare, Co. Antrim

A local lady, Mary McAnulty often used the path to reach the shore so that she could collect dulse (seaweed). As she rested she noticed, in the twilight the figure of a man approaching her. He was limping and looked very pale. He joined her on her way towards the lough and she noticed that he did not speak with a local accent. They rested again near the lough and that is when she noticed that his hair was turning green. When she asked him why, he replied that it was because he had lived for so long beneath the waters of Lough Dhu.

Mary became alarmed at this and he then rested his head on her bag of dulse saying that he was tired. Looking around, she noticed that one of his feet was the shape of horse's hoof. She managed to make her escape and ran as fast as she could until she had almost reached her home. She then heard a dreadful noise, a neighing coming from the Lough. Mary had encountered the devil horse and from then on never used that path again so late in the day!

The Hound of Iskaheen, Co. Donegal

Iskaheen lies north of Muff about ten miles north of the City of Derry in the eastern side of the Inishowen Penisula. A young man from Derry was courting a local girl and they would often go out walking in the area known as Grainne's Gap. One particular evening, he edged his girlfriend to the side of the road. She asked him what he was doing and he replied that he was worried about the massive dog that was approaching them. She could not see anything and when she started to tease him, she noticed how frightened he was and how his eyes were fixed on something ahead.

After a short time, he turned and still white-faced asked if she had seen the dog, which he described in great detail. It was like an Irish wolfhound and as it approached him at great speed, he noticed its large sad eyes before it suddenly disappeared into thin air. The couple made their way home and when she told her father the story he was able to relate an old folklore story of that area. It was said that the 'phantom hound' was the favourite of Eoin the son of Niall of the Nine Hostages who was the local chieftain. After Eoin died, he was buried at Iskaheen in the old Celtic graveyard. After he passed away, his hound is still searching for his former master.

The Headless Horse of Mullenakill, Co. Armagh

Mullenakill lies in the parish of Killyman in North Armagh and gets its name from 'Mullachna Coille' which means 'the hilltop of the wood'.

When Sir. William Verner went to serve in the Napoleonic Wars, he took his beloved steed Constantine with him. Unfortunately, they were caught up in an explosion and his horse's head was blown off. Sir. William took the remains of the horse home to Mullenakill to be buried. Its ghost is said to roam the area and the sound of its hooves can be heard of an evening.

Haunted House in Moneymore, Co. Derry

Moneymore is a plantation village in mid-Ulster. Its name is derived from 'Muine Mór' meaning 'large thicket or hill'. Within the Rockview Park Estate, it is claimed that one particular house was haunted and strange noises inside frightened away a previous tenant. Some claimed that it was built on top of an old horse's graveyard and the house was used for occult practices. Calls were made for the house to be demolished.

The Black Dog of Morghen, Co. Antrim

Other tales of a ghostly black dog were recorded from Morghen, Co. Antrim. The dog was as big as a pony with red eyes and large fangs which it bares as it prowls around the area at night. Anyone who encounters the dog will become afflicted or have a nervous breakdown.

One young farmer was cycling home near the Elbow Forest at night and knowing the tale, he peddled as fast as he could. Something warned him he was not alone and he soon realised that a giant black dog was running alongside him. The faster he peddled, the faster the dog ran. At a location called Watkin's End, and to the young man's relief, the dog suddenly disappeared!

Another story of the black dog involved a group of travellers who were drinking one night in the village pub. One was left behind and was forced to walk home the few miles to his encampment. On the way, the black dog appeared in front of him, however, the traveller was not frightened as he had consumed quite an amount of drink. He attempted to pat the dog but then realised that it was not an ordinary dog! The dog was getting bigger and bigger and its red eyes were glowing red.

The traveller decided to run for his life and the dog followed him. When the traveller was found much later, he was speaking gibberish, his clothes were in tatters and his face was a mass of cuts and bruises.

Father Hegarty's Rock, Lough Swilly, Co. Donegal

Another ghost story from Lough Swilly is from the spot known as Father Hegarty's Rock at Porthaw. During the Penal Times of the late 17th Century, the saying of masses was strictly forbidden, however, Father Hegarty continued to serve his followers and hid in a small near by cave. He was ambushed while saying mass and made his escape on a horse into Lough Swilly. Unfortunately, he was captured and then beheaded by British Forces in 1711.

Fr. Hegarty's Rock, Buncrana, Co. Donegal

It is claimed that his severed head bounced eight times along the top of the rock before falling into the sea. The marks of the bounce are still to be seen at Porthaw where no signs of greenery have appeared since. Father Hegarty was buried at the site of his death and he is said to have been the last priest to be killed during the Penal Law period. His grave is located on the shore walk between Porthaw and Stragill Beaches, two kilometres from Buncrana.

During the 1990s, four young boys were speeding in their quads along the path dangerously close to the cliff edge where there was a sheer drop of forty feet. All of a sudden a ghostly vision of a white horse appeared in front of them forcing the boys to stop in their tracks. Rearing up on its hind legs, it then jumped off the cliff to the rocks below but after that it of suddenly disappeared. The vision of the horse actually saved the boys from certain injury or even death. The boys were very shocked by this incident and found it difficult to relate. Was this the ghost of Father Hegarty's horse sent to warn the boys?

Fr. Hegarty's Grave, Buncrana, Co. Donegal

This Plaque Marks The Spot
Where In Penal Times
FRIAR SEAMUS HEGARTY, O.P.
Was Beheaded In 1711,
After Surrendering To British Forces.
Born In 1649.
Ordained By Oliver Plunket At Dundalk In 1672.
FRIAR HEGARTY Was P.P. In Fahan
From 1704 Until His Death.

The Wolfhound of Antrim Castle

At the entrance of the castle, there was a stone statue of a large wolfhound. The story goes that if an enemy approaches, the statue will come to life and start to bark very loudly to warn the occupiers. It would then turn back to stone. The statue will never be removed as it is seen to protect the castle.

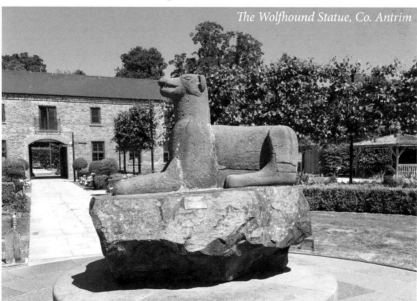

The Wolfhound Statue, Co. Antrim

A 17th Century story is told that a large wolfhound came to the aid of Sir Hugh Clotworthy's wife Marian when she was threatened by a wolf while out walking in the woods. She fainted and when she came to the wolf was dead and the wolfhound was limping and injured. She managed to get the dog back to the castle where she tended to its wounds and brought the animal back to health. The wolfhound then disappeared. When Sir Hugh was out with his men, they heard a large growl and bark coming from the woods. His men were sent to investigate and found a troop of enemies who were ready to attack the castle.

Sir Hugh was convinced that it was the same wolfhound, which had saved his wife and was now protecting the castle. He then built a stone statue to commemorate the hound in 1612. When someone was cleaning the statue, its tail was broken off and soon after the castle was burned to the ground. The statue is now located in the Antrim's Castle Gardens.

The Stables of Tempo Manor, Co. Fermanagh

There is a legend that one of the local Maguire family, the local landowners, asked one of his stable hands to injure a horse belonging to a racing opponent. The stable hand refused and Maguire then murdered him. His ghost is said to haunt the old stable and panics any horse, which is kept there.

The Phantom Coach and Horses of Roskeen, Co. Tyrone

Roskeen lies in the southwest of Lough Neagh. The Dublin to Coleraine coach would have passed through the village of Roskeen before it was re-routed on to the Ferry Road out of Maghery. Those living along the old route claimed to have heard the sound of horses' hooves and the clatter of the coach's metal wheels as it was driven through the village at night.

A similar story exists around Killeshandra, Co. Cavan where a coach pulled by ghostly horses is said to appear when a death is due.

The White Horse Hotel, Co. Derry

The Whitehorse Hotel is supposed to be haunted by a complete mail stagecoach and its portly driver. The coach pulls up at the hotel and the driver is supposed to leave the coach and enter the hotel where he mysteriously disappears!

Dundermot Mound, the Gateway to Hell, Ballymena

Dundermot Mound is actually an ancient fort north of Glarryford, Ballymena. Its name is derived from 'Dún Diarmada' meaning 'Dermot's Fort'. It has a mystical past and has been described as one of the 'Secret Gateways to Hell' by a local historian when interviewed on Radio Ulster's 'Your Place and Mine' programme.

It is said that when the mound opens, all the forces of hell are released and anyone nearby will be sucked into the underworld and never seen again.

The story goes back to 1798 during the United Irishmen's Rebellion and an important cargo had to be delivered to an army barracks in Derry. A coach and horses set out from Belfast and along the way, a great storm blew up. The coach driver, who had his young daughter with him, was called Thomas Meharg and if he delivered the cargo within two days, he was set to receive a substantial bonus.

He was last seen leaving Cullybacky where he had asked, *"Is the bridge at Glarryford down?"* Despite warnings, he continued on his hazardous journey and decided to take a detour and cross the river near the Dundermot Mound.

Legend states that the Mound opened up and swallowed the entire coach and horses and Meharg and his young daughter were never seen again. However, the phantom coach and four horses have been seen and the ghostly driver with his young daughter beside him will ask, *"Is the Bridge at Glarryford Still Up?"* Any answer given will ensure death within the year!

The Phantom Coach and Horses of Antrim Castle

There is a legend that a ghostly coach pulled by four horses appears every year on 31st May. The coach then disappears as it sinks into the large pond in the grounds of the castle. This is in fact a reenactment of a tragic accident, which happened many years ago on this date.

The Galloping Coach, Portaferry, Co. Down

It is claimed that just before midnight on Christmas Eve, when there is a full moon and a clear sky, the sound of galloping horses hooves can be heard speeding along the road between Portaferry and Cloughy. Those that have seen it describe the four dark horses and it appears that the base of the wheels and the horses' legs are beneath the surface of the road.

The coach lurches along as if the road is very bumpy resembling the roads of former years. The coach and horses stop at the vicarage and a pale lady in a long voluptuous dress and a large hat can be seen being helped out of the carriage into the house. She appears to be dressed for a ball but is very sad. After some time, a sad cry can be heard and the pale lady is seen leaving the house, getting back into the coach and heading back into the town again.

As to who this lady is no one knows nor why she should she stop at the vicarage on Christmas Eve.

The White Gates, Ballymena, Co. Antrim

The 'White Gates' is an old house down a lane and just off the Crebilly Road in Ballymena. The area is well known as being haunted. Some years ago, a robbery occurred at the house and the robber rode off towards the gates at the end of the lane. Guards were waiting on him and had stretched a wire across the lane so that his head was de-capitated. It is said that each Halloween at midnight, one can hear the sound of horses' hooves and a headless horseman riding towards the 'White Gates'.

The Infamous Galloper Thompson, Belfast

This is one of the most famous of the ghost stories in Belfast and was based on an actual 19th Century person called Gordon Thompson.

Gordon was quite an eccentric gentleman who had returned to live in Belfast after many years touring the world and was a member of Belfast Town Council in 1849. He later returned to Australia where he died in Melbourne in 1886 at the age of eighty-seven years. He had always stated to his friends that after he died, if he did not go to heaven, he would return to his home in Belfast and haunt it. The house was called Jennymount and indeed, several years later, a number of people claimed to have seen a ghost riding a horse through Jennymount Avenue. As Gordon Thompson used to ride his horse in such a way, it was claimed that this was his ghost and the ghost was named 'Galloper Thompson'. It was also said that both the horse and its rider were headless!

Even when Jennymount was demolished and Jennymount Avenue was redeveloped as Alexander Park Avenue, his ghost was still seen in the area. Some people claimed to have been knocked over by the speeding horse.

It was said that there would be three blasts from a hunting horn at midnight and then a horse would disappear from its stable. The next morning, the horse, even though it was back in the stables was in a dirty and exhausted state as if it had been out all night. What had happened overnight was a mystery.

The story of Galloper Thompson certainly kept children off the streets late at night in North Belfast!

Chapter 8

Haunted Places Throughout Ulster

The Dark Hedges, Co. Antrim

The Dark Hedges are situated on the Bregagh Road, on the A147, approximately two miles from the village of Stranocum (between Dervock and Armoy) in County Antrim. They consist of a beautiful avenue of beech trees, which were planted in the 18th Century by the Stuart family, wealthy local landowners who lived nearby in Gracehill House. The magnificent trees were planted to impress visitors as they approached the entrance to their mansion, which is now a golf club. Some two centuries later, the iconic trees remain as an outstanding natural phenomenon in N. Ireland and are included in a list of the twelve best road trips in the U.K.

In recent times, the two hundred year old beech trees have been used in the filming of HBO's epic series The Game of Thrones where in Season 2, Episode 1; they represented 'The King's Road'. The Character Arya Stark had escaped from her enemies in King's Landing, disguised as a boy and hidden in a cart. She is with Yores,

Gendry, Hot Pie and others who are to join the Night's Watch, travelling north on the King's Road.

The Dark Hedges, Co. Antrim

Legend states that the Dark Hedges are haunted by 'A Grey Lady' who appears after dusk and is seen wandering through the trees before she finally disappears at the very last one. Some say she is the ghost of a member of the Stuart family who fell in love with one of the stable hands. Her family did not approve of the relationship and the young couple decided to elope. Unfortunately, she fell down the stairs of the family home and died from her injuries. She had always dressed in grey and it is her ghost – the 'Grey Lady' who is believed to haunt the area. Employees have claimed to have seen her in the house and on one occasion, she is supposed to have appeared before a car on the driveway, causing it to crash into a nearby tree.

Some say that the Grey Lady is the ghost of a maid in the Gracehill House who died in mysterious circumstances while others state that she is in fact a lost spirit from an old nearby former graveyard and only wishes to remain remembered. The graveyard awakens each Halloween and the forgotten souls re-emerge from their graves.

Over the years, there have been many reported stories of the Grey Lady appearing to individuals. One story concerned a couple that was driving through the hedges late at night when their car had a puncture. The couple both got out of the car and the wife held a torch while here husband replaced the tyre. She accidentally dropped the torch and suddenly in the eerie darkness they heard this strange whistling noise before a glowing grey light descended on the area. Out of the grey mist, a thin, pale lady emerged, floating off the ground and with the darkest of eyes. The couple immediately started to run but the lady followed and when the husband tripped on the road, she reached out and grabbed his wrist. He tried to escape again but her grip was too strong and he was lifted off the ground as she whispered something in his ear. He turned a deathly shade of white and fell to the ground while the lady moved into the trees and disappeared.

Somehow the couple managed to get back to their car and they noticed that a handprint was burned into the man's wrist. He refused to tell his wife what the lady had said to him earlier. It was many years later that he finally revealed her words, *"When you die, you will be mine"*. His wife reassured him that he had many years left and it was nonsense. However, with a frightened look, he added that the lady's last sentence was, *"Forty isn't that far away"*. The man was soon to be forty!

A reputed image has been also captured of the Grey Lady by a local photographer.

Rathlin Island, Co Antrim

Rathlin Island is Northern Ireland's only inhabited island located five miles north of Ballycastle on the North Antrim Coast. Reached by a regular ferry, it offers a dramatic coastal scenery with rugged terrain, towering sea cliffs and a diverse wildlife. Legend states that Rathlin Island was created by Finn Mac Cool's mother. Apparently, she walked off to Scotland to get some whiskey as her son Finn had drunk Ireland dry! In her apron, she carried some soil, which she threw in front of her to make a path. Unfortunately, she tripped and all the soil fell into the sea to create the island of Rathlin with her trapped underneath! There is a local saying that when a storm is raging, *'the oul wirch is kickin'*. Legend states that a Fairy Island appears every seven years in the sea between Rathlin and Ballycastle.

Over one hundred and fifty people live on the island among its many ruined cottages and dry stonewalls. The island is approximately 2.5 miles (4 km) by 4 miles (6 km) and has the shape of a reversed 'L'.

Rathlin has had a varied history and a rich cultural heritage with one of the first recorded attacks by the Vikings in Ireland in the 8th Century when many people were killed and churches were burnt. In 1306, Robert the Bruce, the so-called 'King of the Scots', sought refuge in Rathlin following his defeat by King Edward. It is claimed that while he was here, he hid in a cave where he noticed a spider, which tried several times to build a web across two rocks. This courageous attempt gave Bruce the incentive to make a further attempt at winning the crown eventually succeeding at the battle of Bannockburn in 1314. Some say Bruce and his men are still on the island- trapped by a spell, as they lie sleeping in a cave on the site of the former castle. Once the spell is broken, they will rise up and re-unite Rathlin with Scotland.

Rathlin Island Plaque

Other invasions and massacres occurred in the 16th Century when the earl of Essex ordered Francis Drake and John Norreys to the island to deal with Scottish refugees from the Clan MacDonnell. Hundreds of men, women and children were slaughtered. Local people claim that the cries of the children as they were been snatched from their mothers' arms can still be heard. Many watched from 'Cnocknacriedin Hill' as their men folk were slaughtered in the fields below. The Hill is now known as the 'Hill of the Screaming'. In 1642, soldiers were ordered to kill the Catholic MacDonalds and once again many hundreds were massacred with the women thrown off the high cliffs into the sea.

With such a dark and sad history, it is no surprise that Rathlin has so many ghosts and spirits. One story was told by a local fisherman who, along with a group of other fishermen, set out very early one morning. They agreed to take a break and securing their boat they went inside one of the caves along the western shore of the island. One of the group noticed an opening at the back of the cave, which they had never observed before. Entering it, the cave opened into another empty space where they decided to remain, light a fire and make their tea.

It was only when the men were reaching out their mugs for their share, that the man with the kettle froze. He looked terrified and it was then realized that although there was five of them, there was six sets of hands held out! An extra mug had appeared out of the darkness and the nearest fisherman could feel someone breathing beside him- some unknown person!

One of the group whispered, *"Finish pouring the tea"* and with his hand still shaking, this task was eventually completed. When the extra mug was filled, the mystery hand withdrew into the darkness once again. When the group looked back, there was nothing there. No one has been able to explain this strange event and only that there were so many witnesses, it is hard to believe. No one has stayed in that cave ever since.

The Piper's Cave, Ballintra, Co. Donegal

Ballintra lies between Donegal Town and Ballyshannon. Its name is derived from 'Baile an tSratha' meaning 'the town beside the beach'. Another haunted cave lies within the natural limestone caves called 'the Pullans' through which the Ballintra River flows. One of the caves is said to be haunted by a wandering musician, who seeking shelter from a storm one night, entered the cave system never to be seen again.

In the 1920s, another storm relocated a large beech tree further down the stream but its roots continued to grow and spread out through the rocks. A group of botanists later discovered a human skull embedded within the roots as they passed down through the cave. Further examination revealed the skull to be over 400 years old - perhaps belonging to the missing musician.

It is claimed that on calm moonlight nights, one can hear the distant drone of pipes echoing from the haunted chamber which has become known as the Piper's Cave.

Blue Lady of Tollymore Forest, Newcastle, Co. Down

Tollymore Forest lies on the outskirts of Newcastle and its name is derived from 'Tulaigh Mhór' meaning 'large mound'.

The 'Blue Lady Ghost' is said to haunt the Forest Park at Tollymore. Apparently, the lady used to live in the old seat of the Roden family in Tollymore House. Her former home was demolished after the war. She wanders restlessly now looking for her old home and she has been seen gliding up and down the tree-lined avenue.

Tollymore has been used as a filming location for Westeros in the Game of Thrones including the Campfire scene in the haunted forest when Trion and Jon talk on their way north to the Wall. Also the Wolfswood near Winterfell, The Kingroad near Castle

Black and a Forest near The Dreadfort. The picturesque Altavaddy
Bridge was used when the Starks found the Direwood Pups and
of the Campling Pit where The Night's Watch find dismembered
bodies in the snow.

Tullymore Forest, Newcastle, Co.Down

Bogey Hill, Newcastle, Co. Down

Newcastle is located where 'the Mountains of Mourne Sweep down
to the Sea' and Bogey Hill overlooks Newcastle Harbour. Back in
1843, there was a tragic fishing disaster and many local men were
drowned at sea. It is said that one of the widow's has been seen
grieving for her lost husband on Bogey Hill. She is dressed in black
and as she looks out to sea, she sobs for her long lost husband.

Strange Sightings on Cavehill, Belfast

Cavehill lies above the city of Belfast and its three caves and the
surrounding area were inhabited as far back as the Iron Age. Both
Belfast Zoo and Belfast Castle attract visitors to the area but in the
early 1900s, stories of a ghostly wailing noise and even sightings
attracted many of the city's inhabitants to investigate and see if
they could also spot a ghost.

In 1915, a couple was out for a walk when they observed what appeared to be a floating man move towards them. The couple ran for their lives and disregarded any brambles in their path. The man had to be later treated for cuts and bruises. The same ghostly image was reported by several others. One of the caretakers from the Castle saw a man staring at the trees, and thinking he was a poacher, he shouted at him but the man ignored him. Closer inspection revealed that the man was floating about two feet off the ground. The caretaker ran back to the castle and he and his work colleague locked themselves inside until the next morning.

In 1922, another couple came across a human skeleton exactly where the previous sightings occurred. The police identified it as belonging to a John Scott who had disappeared years ago. He was a tailor originally from Waringstown and had his own business in Belfast. It is likely that he had committed suicide on the Cavehill. After his remains were buried, the ghostly sightings stopped.

The Ghosts of Drumbeg, Lisburn

Drumbeg lies outside Lisburn and is considered by many as one of the most haunted places in Ireland. Its first church dated from the 13th Century. Over the centuries, the area suffered many tragedies including the plague and the famine. Highwaymen would have quite active on this busy route outside Belfast and at one time there were gallows erected on the bridge at Drumbeg. During the 18th Century, a woman was whipped the whole five miles from Lisnagarvey to Drumbridge as punishment for her crimes.

The ghost of an old beggar woman has been seen on the bridge. She is very haggard and carries the starving body of a baby. Some say it is the ghost of a highwayman who killed her and the baby before he was later executed for all his crimes. Her ghost walks along the road and appearing out of a nearby wall as well as on the road itself when she has suddenly appeared in front of a startled driver.

The most famous ghost of Drumbeg is that of James Haddock. When James died in 1657, he left part of his land to his wife Arminell and the rest to his son when he became twenty-one years of age. One of James's executors was Daniel Davis and he later married the widow Arminell and they had another son. Daniel managed to alter the will so that this second son became the main beneficiary instead of James's son.

Some years later, one of James's friends, Francis Tavener, was out riding one night when his horse suddenly reared up and there was the ghost of James Haddock who uttered these words. *"Take Daniel Davis to court. There is something strange happening to my will"*.

Daniel did as he was told and court proceedings were started. On the day of the court, the room was packed. The blinds were drawn and in the gloom, the court usher shouted, *"Call James Haddock"*. As the crowd held their breath, the usher repeated the call and slowly a hand, draped in a shroud, arose from the witness box and a disembodied voice boomed out, *"Is this enough?"* The crowd erupted and satisfied that Francis Taverner was telling the truth, the case against Daniel Davis was proved and he was found guilty.

James Haddock was buried in the graveyard at Drumbeg Parish Church. It is said that his headstone never stays upright and always falls over when re-erected.

Another Drumbeg Ghost Story was told in 'Ulster Ghosts' in the Irish Monthly back in 1929 by W. Moore.

The story involved a Lady Ghost with a grievance. She had been murdered by persons who were committing a robbery. There was a witness to the murder but this man did not come forward with the evidence to convict her killers.

Her ghost started to appear to this witness on the same day at the same time each week. She would drag the poor man to a nearby field where she lectured him about her 'ghostly troubles' and the fact that he should have come forward.

One particular Sunday, she appeared three times. The poor man decided to call in his neighbours for help. The ghost did not care and despite his neighbours holding him down, she was still able to drag him into the field once again. Once again, she lectured him about her need for revenge and the punishment that should be given to her attackers.

Eventually, the witness gave in and came forward with his evidence. Her killers were apprehended and then sentenced. Her ghost never appeared again!

Mystery Man in Slievenaman, Mourne Mountains, Co. Down

Some years ago, five hill walkers were exploring the hills around Spelga Dam and as they clambered over Slievenaman, one of the walkers fell and was injured. The rest of the group managed to carry him to a nearby cottage where he could shelter while they went for help. A fire was lit in the old hearth and he was made as comfortable as possible. While the hill walker remained in the cottage and waited for help, he had a visitor. It was an elderly man who kept him company and chatted to him for several hours. The hill walker then fell asleep.

Eventually, the others came back with help. They asked if he had been lonely waiting for them and he told them about the old man who had now vanished. They asked if he knew who this mystery companion was and he described him. One of the party of helpers was a local man and he became very surprised at hearing the description. It was another local Slievenaman resident who had died a couple of years earlier. Everyone, especially the injured hill walker was very surprised to hear this.

The Friar's Bush Graveyard, Belfast

Many stories exist of haunted graveyards throughout Ulster. One such graveyard is Friar's Bush in Belfast's University Area where frequent sightings of ghosts have been recorded. Its history goes back to the 5th Century. During the cholera outbreak in the middle of the 19th Century, hundreds of bodies were buried here in a mass grave and their ghosts remain restless due to the lack of a holy burial. Another story concerns a tunnel, which runs underneath the graveyard. During the late 19th Century, a worker in the tunnel kept reporting how unseen hands were touching him. To this day many university staff refuse to enter the tunnel.

The Green Lady of Vicar's Hill, Co. Armagh

For many years the story of the 'Green Lady' has struck fear into children in the City of Armagh. Children were warned to get home before dark before the 'Green Lady' would appear.

Vicar's Hill is a small street of terraced houses, just opposite St. Patrick's Cathedral. The 'Green Lady' tale is based on a true event from 1888.

Vicar's Hill, Co. Armagh

One of the street's residents was the Prior family. Mrs. Prior was the widow of an army colonel and she had two daughters at home, Bellina and Adele. Bellina Prior had been acting strange for some time and was prone to fainting fits. She was left alone one day with a neighbour's child, four-year old Ann Slavin and when her mother and sister returned to the house, Bellina was in the living room but the child was found drowned in a downstairs water boiler. There are various versions of what she said had happened but she was arrested and charged with murder.

Bellina claimed that the child's death was an accident and that she had not been able to save her as she had 'lost her presence of mind'. At the court case, Bellina was found guilty of murder but insane. While she was in prison, she had attempted suicide and was then sent to a 'lunatic asylum', firstly in Armagh and then Dublin. Her family also left Armagh and moved to Dublin and when Bellina was released into her mother's care they remained in Dublin. Unfortunately, her body and that of her mothers were discovered dead in November 1909. Both of them were poisoned and Bellina's mother had left a suicide note….. *"I destroy my daughter that no one may get to her and do away with myself immediately after"*. A tragic end to a tragic story!

Back in Armagh, their story became twisted and exaggerated over the years with people scared to go near the house in Vicar's Hill. The myth grew of a lady who was a child killer and whose soul had been captured in a green bottle and hidden in a bricked up window in her old house. The ghostly 'Green Lady' has been feared ever since and acted as a warning for children in the area to get home safely before dark.

The Old Railway Bridge, Sion Mills. Co. Tyrone

This old bridge is mainly used by pedestrians out walking their dogs but is claimed that the bridge is haunted. Unfortunately, some people have used it to take their own lives by falling into the river below. A number of people have seen a ghostly figure emerge from the water below, it stands around for a while before walking back into the river.

Ballyboley Forest, Larne, Co. Antrim

The name Ballyboley is derived from 'Baile na Bnaile' meaning the 'townland of the summer milking place'.

Strange stories have been told about this forest for many years where people have disappeared and shadowy figures have been seen among the trees. It is believed to have been an ancient Druid site as there are many stone formations and circular trenches in the ground. Some believe that the forest contains 'old Celtic footpaths' and a 'gateway' to 'the Otherworld'.

In the 1990s, a young couple while walking through the woods, were scared out of their wits when they observed thick black smoke and screaming voices near them. In the same decade, another story was reported in the local newspaper. Two men heard a strange flapping sound and then a woman apparently moaning in pain. They ran to the spot where the sound was coming from and discovered that the trees there were covered in blood but no sign of the lady. The strange flapping sound increased so they made a run for it. One of the men looked back to see four figures dressed in brown rags and with their heads covered. The figures were definitely not there before.

Main Street, Ballymoney, Co. Antrim

There is an old story of a ghost who walks up and down the main street of Ballymoney at midnight every Friday 13th and also at Halloween. It is the ghost of a local man George 'Bloody' Hutchinson dragging a large metal ball which is chained to his ankle. It is said that if anyone tries to stop Bloody Hutchinson's ghost, his spirit will be banished forever.

George was a local magistrate and played an active role in suppressing the United Irishmen Rebellion of 1798. He sentenced Alexander Gamble to death by hanging at the clock tower at the top of Main Street.

Two other United Irishmen met the same fate but they were hung on top of a hill at Dungorbery, which is a townland near Ballymoney. (Dungorbery is derived from Dún gCairbre' meaning 'Cairbre's Fort').

George was buried in an old graveyard in Ballymoney Town, which is apparently also haunted. One local man was dared to spend the night in the graveyard. He managed to achieve this but when he appeared the next morning, he was naked, his hair was white and he was talking gibberish about the 'ghosts'.

The Ghost of Emyvale. Co. Monaghan

Emyvale is an anglicised version of the former name 'Sarnageeragh' meaning 'shallow ford of the sheep'. It is a village on the main Dublin to Derry road.

The ghost of an old man is said to roam up and down the main street in Emyvale. He moans continually and calls out the name *"Mary"*. The story goes that Mary was his wife and she was murdered on this street by robbers some two hundred years previously.

The Famous Finnis 'Ghost Tree', Dromara, Co. Down

In the early part of the 20th Century, an evil spirit haunted the area around the Dree Hill Road Bridge, which spans the River Lagan in the townland of Finnis, Dromara. All the villagers were terrified to go near the bridge at any time of the day or night. Eventually, the local priest took it upon himself to try to exorcise the ghost and he actually managed to capture it into a large bottle. Near the bridge, there is a hollow sycamore tree and the priest hid the bottle inside.

After the exorcism, the bridge was indeed free of the evil spirit and everyone was relieved. As to the tree itself, no one would touch it nor allow anyone else to touch it. Even when overhead lines were being erected and the tree was due to be felled, the villagers protested and the priest had to be called to stop the workers from cutting it down. The power lines were run through the tree's upper branches.

So the tree remained on the bridge but it died and still no one had the courage to remove it in case the evil spirit, which was bottled up, inside was disturbed. However, the forces of nature caused its downfall. Part of the tree was broken off during a storm, the branches lay where they fell and in 2009 another storm toppled the tree over. But the whereabouts of the bottle and the evil spirit bottled up inside are unknown.

Biddy, the Ghost of Smithfield Market, Belfast

Biddy Farrelly is said to haunt the area around Gresham Street and the Castlecourt Shopping Centre.

It is said that Biddy was involved romantically with Luke White, a local businessman who ran a successful bookshop in Smithfield Market. When Luke moved away to Dublin and Biddy became broken hearted. She started to drown her sorrows in alcohol to try to forget about Luke. When Luke, unfortunately, died suddenly and he left Biddy a legacy. However, Biddy's drinking became worse. In fact, she drank herself to death believing that one day she would be reunited with Luke in the afterlife.

Unfortunately, this did not happen and instead Biddy's ghost still walks around the market looking for her one and only love.

Olivands Hill, Magherafelt. Co. Derry

Many years ago, Olivands Hill was the highest point overlooking the town of Magherafelt. The large oak trees there were used for the public hangings of criminals who were sentenced to death. Much later on, a young local lady became pregnant but was unmarried. She became very depressed and in the end took her own life on the hill as she was so ashamed of her predicament.

Her ghost is said to haunt the grounds but also the old farmhouse nearby. A number of families moved into the house over the years but they all quickly abandoned it as they were unable to stay due to the haunting. The house lay empty for years and eventually when another family moved in, the sightings became less frequent. The house is no longer here, however, the ghost of a crying lady dressed in grey has been seen in the area.

The Castle Hole, Castlederg, Co. Tyrone

The Derg River is renown for its salmon fishing yet it reputedly contains a dangerous vortex called the Castle Hole.

There is a legend that there was a tunnel built from the castle underneath the river to allow an escape route. One night a piper decided to go down the tunnel on his own. Even though he continued to play his pipes so that he could be found easily if he got lost, the music suddenly stopped and he was never seen again. The tunnel then caved in, and the piper's body was never recovered.

It is said the locals still hear the sound of mysterious piping around the castle. No one can trace the origin and it is believed to be the ghost of the missing piper.

The Ballyroney Lake Ghost, Co. Down

Ballyroney is a rural area in south Co. Down a few miles outside Rathfriland. It gets its name from 'Baile Uí Ruanadha' which means 'O'Roney's townland'.

Ballyroney Lake, Co. Down

Many years ago a brother and sister lived together in a farm at Ballyroney. They were very attached to one another and neither wanted anything more from life than the happy companionship and goodwill, which they shared.

However, a young man came into the girl's life and he fell in love with her. She of course was thrilled and returned this love. They planned to get married and perhaps then move to a different locality. Her brother forbade her to marry her fiancé and in fact he did not allow her to see him again. The girl was broken hearted and as the days, months and years rolled on, she became thin and listless. By this time her unfortunate young fiancé had emigrated. At last, the girl could go on no longer and one night she crept out and drowned herself in Ballyroney Lake.

Her brother was to pay in more ways than one for his callous action. His sister's ghost haunted him every night till at length he went to the Scotch Harvest in the hope that going to a different country would 'lay the ghost'. However, while he was on the ship, his sister continued to haunt him, even throughout the whole harvest. When he sailed back to Ireland, his sister's ghost returned with him. He knew now that it was quite hopeless to think of peace again. He was an absolute bundle of nerves and so eventually one night he too went down to the Lake in Ballyroney and drowned.

The Lough Swilly Ghost, Co. Donegal

Lough Swilly gets its name from 'Suile' meaning 'Lake of Sorrows'. Many people have lost their lives in the Lough, which lies in the North East of the county. Buncrana lies on the eastern shore of Lough Swilly and is about sixteen miles northwest from the City of Derry on the Inishowen Peninsula. Buncrana gets it name from Bun Cranncha meaning 'foot of the (river) Crana'.

One such sad story is that of two young men whose boat was capsized when it struck some rocks beyond Buncrana. They managed to cling to the rocks for a while until one of them decided to swim ashore and get help while the other young man shouted as loud as he could. Someone heard the shouts and that young man was rescued but the other perished. His mother was distraught and walked up and down the shore weeping and wailing until his body was finally pulled from the sea.

People say that on stormy nights, one can hear shouts and crying on that beach and a light has been seen in the location of the rocks.

The Ghostly Boy, Giant's Causeway, Co. Antrim

The Giant's Causeway is one of the most famous of all places in N. Ireland being one of the natural wonders of the world. Legend states that it was built by Finn McCool as a walkway to Scotland. This ghostly tale involved a family from Belfast who travelled by train to the Giant's Causeway for a summer's day outing in 1910. There were many visitors at the Causeway so the family moved away from the main section so that they could have a picnic.

The Giant's Causeway, Co. Antrim

After they had eaten, the mother and father took a nap and left their maid to look after the children especially a boy aged nine who was warned to be careful as he jumped over the rock formations. The mother suddenly woke up calling out his name *"Something has happened!"* she cried. Her maid assured her that she had just seen the boy but when they all got up he could not be seen and they hurried down to the sea. There was no sign of him.

Help was summoned but still there was no sign of the child until a few days later when his body was found about three miles further along the coast. It was concluded that he had slipped into the sea and drowned.

Soon after this terrible tragedy, reports came in from people who had seen a small boy in a sailor suit down by the water's edge. On one occasion, he was asked if he was lost. The people concerned noticed how deadly pale he was and that his clothes were soaking wet. He simply vanished after that. Since then several more sightings of the boy have been seen on the rocks.

Mystery Figure in Omagh, Co. Tyrone

The following story was reported in the Dublin Daily Express in 1912 and concerned Patrick Hunter who was the night watchman in the town at that time. He claimed to have seen a ghost while carrying out his duties. Patrick would often take his dog with him as he walked through the town. As he approached the Abbey Bridge, where there had been a recent mystery drowning, his dog became very frightened and pulled on Patrick's coat to get away. The dog finally bolted off in the opposite direction. Looking at the bridge, he saw what appeared to be a man approaching quite swiftly towards him.

A ghost in the mist

However, as he came closer the man turned to the side towards the edge of the bridge before he disappeared through the iron railings. Patrick was shocked by what he had just seen and looked through the railings but could not see where the man had gone to. He reported the sighting to the local police who also could find no evidence of the mysterious figure. Patrick however was convinced that the apparition was connected to the recent drowning fatality and what he had seen was the ghost of the victim.

Chapter 9

Banshees & Other Death Warnings

'Hast thou heard the Banshee at morn,
Passing by the silent lake,
Or walking the fields by the orchard?
Alas! that I do not rather behold
White garlands in the hall of my fathers.'

The Banshee mournful wails
In the midst of the silent, lonely, lonely night,
Plaining, she sings the song of death…

Ancient Irish Poem

Introduction

Of all the supernatural phenomena, the banshee is the single one that is strongly associated with Ireland and is supposed to foretell the death of some member of the household that she visits. The original banshee (sidhe Bhean) or 'fairy woman' was described as a beautiful young girl from Tir Na nOg. Over the years, her appearance changed to that of an old hag with long hair, which she is seen combing. She appears as pale like a corpse and covered in freckles and with terrible eyes that stare at you with great sadness because of the death that is going to occur. She makes a mournful sound similar to a fox or a cat cry. The keen (caoine) or funeral cry of the peasantry is said to be an imitation of her cry. The banshee was sometimes called 'an bhean chaointe' which means the mourning woman - there are no male banshees.

When more than one banshee comes to cry, the man or woman who is dying must have been very holy or very brave. Sometimes the banshee is accompanied by an immense black coach, mounted by a coffin and drawn by headless horses. The banshee is also seen washing bloody clothing, which is said to belong to the person whose death is near. Because of that she is also known as the 'washer woman'.

She wails, as most people know, over the death of a member of some old Irish families especially those with 'Mc' or 'O' in their surnames. One of the most famous banshees in Irish Folk history was Aibhill who appeared to Brian Boro on the night before the Battle of Clontarf in 1014. Brian knew that he was soon to die. There are also stories of banshees in other countries where certain Irish families have settled.

There is an old warning that if you meet a banshee, you must not look at her, instead look down at the ground. If her eyes meet yours and she recognises your Celtic soul as one of hers, she may throw her comb in your direction and claim you as her next victim.

The Story of Finvola, Dungiven, Co. Derry

Finvola was the beautiful daughter of Dermot, the Chieftain of the O'Cahans from the 17th Century. She fell in love with Angus McDonnell of the clan McDonnell from the western isles of Scotland.

Dermot agreed to the marriage but on the condition that when Finvola died, her remains would be brought back to Dungiven for her burial. Unfortunately, her death came about too soon and Angus could not bear to part with her so buried her near him on the Isle of Islay. Finvola's brothers were out on Benbradagh Mountain when they heard a piercing wail and recognised it as the call of their banshee – Grannie Roe O'Cahan a spirit who only cried for the death of an O'Cahan. They knew that a member of their clan had died and knowing that all were safe and well at home, decided to make the journey to Islay. There they found Angus deep in grief and explained that he could not bring himself to return her remains home. The brothers then brought Finvola home to Dungiven and the banshee's cry was heard no more.

Outside Dungiven Castle is a sculpture named 'The Roe Trilogy' which captures the story of Finvola. The first depicts Finvola in the arms of Angus, the second, the lament of the banshee and the third depicts her brothers in search of her.

The Bard or Harper was an important figure in Celtic Ireland as they sang and told the ancient tales as they travelled throughout the land. One small field in Dungiven is called the 'Harpers' Walk' and was the old site of a School for Harpers. One of the most famous of the O'Cahan harpers was Toal O'Cahan who is said to have composed the ballad 'Finvola, The Gem of the Roe'.

A statue of Finvola outside Dungiven Library, Co. Derry

The Gem of the Roe

In a land of O'Cahan where bleak mountains rise
O'er those brown ridgy tops now the dusky clouds fly
Deep sunk in a valley a wild flower did grow
And her name was Finvola, the Gem of the Roe

For the Isles of Abunde appeared to out view
A youth clad in tartan, it's strange but it's true
With a star on his breast and unstrung was his bow
And he sighed for Finvola the Gem of the Roe

The Gem of the Roe, The Gem of the Roe
And he sighed for Finvola
The gem of the Roe

To the grey shores of Alba his bride he did bear
But short were the fond years those lovers did share
For thrice on the hillside the Banshee cried low
Twas the death of Finvola the Gem of the Roe

No more up the streamlet her maidens will hie
For wan the pale cheek and bedimmed the blue eye
In silent affliction our sorrow will flow
Since gone is Finvola the Gem of the Roe

The Banshee of Newcastle Harbour, Co. Down

A banshee is supposed to haunt Newcastle Harbour in Co. Down and has been seen walking among the tied up boats and lobster pots. She has been heard crying out in a high-pitched voice. This is seen as a warning to the boatmen not to go out to sea, as an impending death is imminent.

The Banshee of the Brandywell, Co. Derry

This story concerns a young boy who was sent to stay at his grandparent's house while his father worked the nightshift. As the grandfather was ill, young John was told that he would fetch his father if his condition deteriorated. John brought some of his friends over to keep him company and on one particular night, they all heard wailing and screeching coming from the back yard of the grandparent's house. Stepping outside they saw nothing but the back door slammed shut behind them. As they made their way around a back lane to the front of the house, they heard the same wailing but coming from the front this time. As the noise became much louder, his friends scattered but John walked on just in time to see his father reach the front door.

They both made it in time to see the old man die. John's grandmother put her arms around him and said, *"You heard the Banshee. Didn't you?"* John started to cry and apologised for not been able to fetch his father sooner. His father hugged him and told him that the banshee had warned him because their family name began with 'Mc'.

The Banshee of Shane's Castle, Antrim

Another banshee called Maeveen, the White Lady of Sorrow, is linked to the O'Neill family in Shane's Castle. She is said to be the daughter of one of the O'Neill's. Her name is derived from 'Iníon Rua' meaning 'the red-haired daughter'. In fact, the O'Neill family would have kept a bedchamber for her sole use in the attic of the castle. Just before a death in the family, the figure of a woman could be seen pacing up and down the room continually wringing her hands and crying. A beautiful figure, she was described as tall and slender with long golden hair and blue eyes and dressed in a long green dress. This happened until the castle was destroyed in the fire of 1816.

One theory for the fire was that when Lord O'Neill decided to put the room to another use, the castle was destroyed. Some say that the O'Neill banshee still appears on moonlight nights wandering under the ancient trees near the castle.

The Rathlin Island Banshee, Co. Antrim

Another banshee story was discovered during our research from Rathlin Island as described by Bob Curran. Neil Craig was sent for the local priest when one of his neighbours became very ill. On their way back to the man's house, they had to go through a bog and that is where Neil heard a strange noise. It started off as a moan and then developed into a sharp cry as if someone was in severe pain. Neil asked the priest if he had heard the cry but he denied it and instead insisted that they hurry on. The noise was heard again and still the priest continued to deny hearing anything but Neil thought his voice was a bit shaky! The priest added that it must have been a fox!

When two men reached the neighbour's house, the man was already dead. After some time, they walked back through the bog once again only this time there were no strange moans or cries to be heard. At the priest's house, they drank two whiskies and Neil noticed that the priest was very pale but still denied hearing anything strange during their walk. After a couple more whiskies, Neil was ready and unafraid to return through the bog once more but he still maintains that this was a banshee wailing the imminent death of his neighbour and the priest simply would not admit to it.

Apparitions before Death

Seeing a person's image can sometimes indicate a death is about to occur. Such images are called 'doppelgangers' and are the double of a living person. The name is of German origin.

The Mourne Doppelganger, Co. Down

In the Mourne area, a farmer was working outside near his home when he saw his elderly mother standing in the yard. When he went inside his house, he asked his ailing mother if she had been outside and she denied it. Felling very uneasy about this and because he knew that the vision he had seen was a warning sign, he immediately went looking for the local priest.

He was lucky to come across the priest quite quickly on the road but when they both returned to the farmhouse, he discovered that his mother was already dead.

Daylight Wraiths

The appearance of a living person, usually far away in another land, to people who know them well, usually indicates that the person is dead or in need of help. Sometimes the figure can be mischievous and display similar activity to that of a poltergeist. One such story is outlined below:-

Daylight Wraith in Cavankirk, Co. Tyrone

Many years ago, a prosperous family lived in the Cavankirk area of the Clogher Valley. However, one son Robert, was always getting into trouble. It was decided that he should leave the area to get away from the trouble he was in and he emigrated to Canada. He left another brother and sister at home on the farm.

Some years later, the sister thought she saw Robert in one of the barns. A neighbour also asked if Robert had returned home as he had also seen him in the area. However, a letter arrived from Canada confirming that he was still there but the family's concerns were raised again when the brother thought he saw Robert near some trees on the farm.

His sister started to notice that some household items were being moved around the house and she also had a feeling that someone was watching her. Even the animals started to behave strangely and one of the cows actually kicked out at her in the byre. That is where she saw her brother Robert again but this time, he looked quite angry. His figure rushed at her and forced her onto the ground and started to put his hands around her throat! She was saved by her brother who heard her screams.

More and more strange things started to happen and then a letter arrived from Canada informing them that Robert had died. The activity around the farm only increased, even his brother was pelted with stones and clods of earth as he walked around the farm. Visitors also noticed the moving objects and heard strange noises.

The local Presbyterian Minister was asked to help and even though he did say prayers and read out passages from the bible, the noises came back that same night but more intensely. The brother and sister were at their wits end and decided that they could no longer remain in the family farm. They sold up and moved to America. Over time, the old house and farm fell into ruin as no one was able to make a living from it.

Boom Hall, Co. Derry

Boom Hall was an 18th Century mansion built by the Alexander family along the banks of the River Foyle. It was named after the wooden boom, which was placed across the river to stop ships getting food to the people of Derry during the siege of 1657. The boom was broken by three ships, the Mountjoy, The Jerusalem and the Phoenix and food was eventually delivered to the starving inhabitants in Derry.

The captain of the Mountjoy was Robert Browning and his wife watched the ships enter the city from the shore. Unfortunately, the captain of the Mountjoy later died from his wounds. It is said that his ghost still haunts the area as he searches for his wife. A ghostly figure of a tall man in military attire has been seen wandering up and down. At the same time, his wife, Lady Jane's ghost has also been seen also searching for her husband in the same area.

Boom Hall, Co. Derry

Boom Hall was built on the site and in its day was one of the grandest houses in the district. The Alexander's had four children including two boys, Robert and Waller and they used to play in the extensive gardens of the estate. When Waller was eight he was sent to stay with his grandparents in Drogheda for the summer months. After several weeks, his grandmother was walking down the grand stairs when she saw Waller playing outside the house. Thinking he was home from his holidays, she was delighted and asked her daughter-in-law when had he returned.

She became confused however when she was told that Waller was still in Drogheda. It was two days later that word came through that Waller had taken ill very suddenly and had died at the same time when he was seen by his grandmother at Boom Hall.

Floating Coffins in Attical, Co. Down

It is claimed that some families in Attical, outside Kilkeel, have an amazing gift of seeing into the future. However, that gift is one that can actually foretell the death of a person. To some readers, this is a burdensome gift and not one that everyone would want.

Their amazing powers involve seeing coffins floating in the night sky. At the house where the coffins stop and revolve to rest in an upright position, will indicate that someone who lives there will die very soon.

One family member can recall seeing two coffins floating in the sky one clear winter's night. The coffins stopped outside a house quite close to where he was standing. The coffins then turned upright. The storyteller was puzzled by this event, as there was no-one living in the house; the family had emigrated to Australia some years before. However, two months later word came through that two members of the family who had moved away had passed away. They were involved in a tragic drowning accident that had actually occurred on the same date that the coffins were seen hovering over their old Attical home.

Apparitions after Death

The Sea Captain's Story, Bunbeg, Co. Donegal

Near Inishiny Bridge, Co. Donegal, the dead body of a sea captain was found washed up on the local shore. He and two other members of his crew had previously rowed ashore to get provisions for his ship which was anchored further out in the bay. Despite warnings from the locals of an impending storm, and anxious to get back to their ship, they rowed back. However, the storm broke and they never reached the ship.

Their small boat and the captain's body remains were found the next morning. His remains were removed further inland for burial. However, soon after the people of the village were gathered in one of the houses when they heard footsteps. They were surprised to who it would be as they were all gathered inside. It was a large uniformed man with a peaked hat. They quickly realised that it was the dead captain standing in the doorway.

One woman screamed but one of the men invited him inside. However, the captain moved back and then disappeared. All the people inside rushed outside but there was no sign of the captain nor where there any footsteps in the sand just outside.

Vampires and Other Deathly Tales

Most cultures have tales of vampires and Ireland is no exception. Stories of vampires existed here long before Hollywood featured them. The legendary 'Dearg Diulai', meaning the 'red-blood sucker' rose from her grave to seduce living men and drain their blood from them. There are also tales of the people of Ossory, an ancient kingdom, who could transform themselves into wolves.

It is said that there is a Co. Monaghan connection to Bram Stoker's 'Dracula' published in 1897. An Irishman, he would have heard many stories including the Churchyard Bride from Errigal Truagh Graveyard as described below. It is known that he visited Monaghan and would have 'The Parting Glance', a tablet in St. Patrick's Church in Monaghan depicting Lady Rossmore-Mary Anne Westenra on her deathbed. One of the main characters in Dracula is Lucy Westenra. The surname is quite unusual-of Dutch origin and has a long association with Monaghan and the Rossmore title.

Errigal Truagh Graveyard, Co. Monaghan

Errigal Truagh Graveyard is situated near Killybrone in Co. Monaghan. It is a very old religious site with an ancient graveyard and the ruins of a medieval church dedicated to St. Muadain, a 6th Century Irish Saint. Most of the headstones are very elaborate from the 18th Century and feature the five mortality symbols – skulls, long bones, coffins, bells and hourglasses. Both Catholic and

Protestant families are buried here and the accumulation of graves over the centuries has resulted in the ground been raised much higher than it was originally.

There is a legend that the graveyard is haunted by a spirit that appears to the families of those that are buried here and it is an omen of death. After a funeral has occurred, the spirit will look for the last person to leave the graveyard. If it is a young man, the spirit takes the form of a beautiful lady and if a young girl is the last to leave, the spirit will become a handsome young man. The spirit will charm its victim by showering it with much affection and then it makes a promise, sealed with a kiss to meet in the same churchyard exactly one month later.

Errigal Truagh Graveyard, Co. Monaghan

Once the victim leaves the graveyard, he or she will remember the story of the spectre and become very ill and after one month will die of a terrible wasting sickness. Their remains are taken to the same graveyard for burial and this fulfills the fatal promise.

The story was made famous by the Irish novelist William Carleton (1794-1869) who visited the area and heard several examples of where the young people had fallen victim to the phantom spectre.

He then wrote a ballad called 'The Churchyard Bride'.

... Again the funeral vice came o'er
The passing breeze, as it wailed before,
And streams of mournful music bore
By the bonnie green woods of Killeevy.

'If I to thy youthful heart am dear,
One month from hence thou wilt meet me here,
Where lay thy bridal Eva's bier',
By the bonnie green woods of Killeevy.

He pressed her lips as the words were spoken,
And his banshee's wail-no far and broken-
Murmured 'Death', as he gave the token,
By the bonnie green woods of Killeevy.

'Adieu! adieu! said this lady bright,
And she slowly passed like a thing of light,
Of a morning cloud, from Sir Turlough's sight,
By the bonnie woods of Killeevy.

Now Sir Turlough has death in every vein,
And there's fear and grief o'er his wide domain,
And golf for those who will calm his brain,
By the bonnie woods of Killeevy...

The month is closed, and Green Truagha's pride,
Is married to death-and, side by side,
He slumbers now with his churchyard bride,
By the bonnie woods of Killeevy.

Abhartach the Irish Vampire, Co. Derry

The following story was described by Patrick Joyce, an Irish historian, in his book 'A History of Ireland' in 1880. It is believed that Bram Stoker, read Joyce's book and published has own 'Dracula' vampire story seventeen years later. Many centuries ago in Ireland, the spilling and drinking of blood in many rituals was not uncommon especially that of animal blood. Even in famine times, blood would have been drunk or mixed with meal to create cakes in order to supplement the population's poor diet. The question is did the tradition of the blood-drinking Irish chieftains and story of Abharach be responsible for the idea for Count Dracula rather than the tale of an Eastern European vampire?

Abhartach was a cruel, deformed and evil chieftain from the 6th Century who practiced black magic and whose story may have influenced Bram Stoker when he wrote his novel about Dracula.

Abtarach's tomb lies in a remote townland of Slaughtavery between Garvagh and Dungiven in Co. Derry. Back in the 5th and 6th Centuries, this area also known as Glenuillin was ruled by chieftains who resided in fortified ancient raths and forts. Abhtarach was one such chieftain and rather than being a fair and generous ruler, he was quite an evil tyrant, and trusted no one, not even his own wife. Convinced that she was having an affair, he climbed out of his bedroom in his castle one night to spy on her and while he crept along the parapet, he fell to his death. He was buried, like other chieftains at that time, standing upright.

However, the following day he returned and demanded that each of his subjects give some of their blood to him on a daily basis so that he could sustain his life. His subjects were terrified of him even when he was a member of the 'living dead' and decided to take matters in hand. Another chieftain called Cathán was asked to finally get rid of Abhartach. Once again he 'slew' the being and buried it as before but the next day Abhartach re-appeared asking for more blood. The deed was repeated but each time Cathán thought he had killed him, Abharach once again appeared.

Finally, Cathán consulted with an old 'holy man' who lived nearby. Cathán was told that it was impossible to kill Abharach as he was now one of the undead, a dearg-diúlaí, meaning, 'red-blood sucker' and who sustained his life by drinking human blood. All that could be achieved was to prevent him returning from the dead. He then gave Cathán the following instructions. He must use a sword made out of a yew tree and the body was to be buried upside down, surrounded by thorns and ash twigs and covered by a heavy stone called a leacht. He warned that if the stone was to be lifted at any later stage, Abharach would be free once again to walk the earth and torture people for their blood. The vampire's burial site has actually given the townland its name- Slaughtaverty, which means 'sepulchral monument of the dwarf' or 'Abharach's leacht'.

Cathán did as he told and constructed a massive tomb over the grave so that it could be clearly seen for miles. Over the years since then, the stones from the tomb have been re-used by local farmers but the slab covering the grave still remains and a large thorn tree has grown over the spot. The site is said to be still 'bad ground' and even though some say there was treasure buried with Abharach, local people will not go near the spot especially after dark.

Recent attempts have been made to clear this land but the tree has proved impossible to cut down as chain saws have broken. The site can be visited and was actually included in the 'Mike Gatiss' episode of 'Who do You Think You Are' series on BBC 1. Mike Gatiss is the writer of the Sherlock and Doctor Who Programmes.

Chapter 10
Devil Related Stories

Dr. Thomas Meredith's 'Sudden and Awful Visitation', Ardtrea, Co. Tyrone

This story concerns a local Church of Ireland Minister in Ardtrea, near Cookstown, Co. Tyrone. Ardtrea is derived from 'Ard Tré' meaning 'Tré's Height'. Tré was an ancient Irish saint.

The rector's sudden death in 1819 at the age of forty-two has been the subject of many stories and speculation over the years especially. Dr. Meredith had lived with his wife and family for a number of years and was known to be a very kind person. The story goes that his governess was disturbed when she began seeing a lady in white appearing around the rector's seven children. Some say this was the ghost of Saint Tré who lived around her in the 5th Century.

Dr. Meredith sought advice and was told to lie in wait for the ghost and shoot it with a silver bullet. He sent his family away for the night and much later shots were heard coming from the house. It was said that he had used ordinary bullets first but these did not work. The poor rector was found seriously wounded and died several days later. He was so shocked and disturbed by what he had seen that he was unable to tell what had happened to him. A monument to Dr. Meredith was erected by his sons and placed inside Ardtrea Church.

The following lines on the monument read: -

'He was summoned from a family
Of which he was eminently endeared
On May 2nd 1819
In the 42nd year of his age
By a sudden and awful visitation
But he knew
That his Redeemer lived'

Monument inside
Ardtrea Church

Another version of the story is that the next morning the servants arrived back at the house first and were confronted by a ghostly devil like figure that made horrible noises through the window at them. One of the servants ran to get the local priest so that he could 'lay' the evil figure. The priest arrived and managed to placate the ghost with a bottle of whiskey and when it was almost finished, the evil being turned into a slippery eel to drink the last drop before the priest could do so. The priest immediately sealed the bottle, made a sign of the Cross on it and later buried in the cellar of Ardtrea Church. It is said that the screams of the devil can be heard some nights trying to get out of the bottle.

Cumber House, Claudy, Co. Derry

Claudy is a village located about six miles southeast of Derry. Its name is derived form 'Clóidigh' which means 'the one who washes the strong flowing one'. Years ago, the Browne family were the owners of Cumber House. They were wealthy landowners and were friendly with the local priests. After the older Mr. Browne died, one of the priests was heard saying that he would be *"burning in the flames of hell"*.

The rest of the Browne family heard this and summoned the priest to explain himself and prove that their father was in hell. Under pressure and very agitated, the priest started to pray even rolling up his trousers and kneeling on his bare knees. The priest then drew a circle on the ground and prayed again. Suddenly, out of the circle appeared flames and the figure of the old man. The priest ran from the house and never returned and the family had to find another priest to banish the 'old man' who had haunted their home ever since that day. The second priest drew a circle around one of the trees in the grounds and ordered the spectre inside. To this day, many people claim to have heard the sound of knocking and scraping coming from inside the tree and few will walk the grounds at night on their own.

The Tale of Stumpie's Brae, Co. Derry

Stumpie's Brae lies between Craigadoes and Lifford on the road from Derry. The story was also known as 'Tom the Toiler'. Mrs. Cecil Frances Alexander, the wife of the Church of Ireland Bishop, was an accomplished poet and the author of several well-known hymns including 'All Things Bright and Beautiful'. She adapted the legend into a poem, which was published in 1859. It was written in Ulster Scots.

> **Have ye heird nae talk of Stumpie's Brae,**
> **Down by the Foyle where a cottage lay?**
> **Come closer to me one and aw**
> **'Till a tell ye how the de'il did call.**

A number of authors including Ken McCormack and have also written about the legend in their publications.

The story is that one night, in the early 1800s, an elderly couple was huddled up against their turf fire while a storm was raging outside their isolated cottage. They were by all accounts a miserable pair and would not think twice about stealing from any passersby who would stop with them. All of a sudden there was a loud bang at their door. It was a pedlar who asked if he could seek shelter from the wind and the rain. Adding that he would pay them well, they immediately invited him into their cottage.

The visitor was a pedlar and was returning from a fair in Derry. As he sat on his bed underneath the stairs, he started to count his takings of the day. It was strange that the visitor's clothes and boots were not wet and muddy but all the couple could think of was how much money they could steal. The pedlar counted out twenty gold sovereigns and the couple decided the gold was theirs!

While he slept, he was attacked and murdered with a pickaxe. The couple then found his purse of gold.

> **'Look at his gold' they cried with delight**
> **And they danced with joy on that evil night.**

They decided to bury his body in a nearby bog. However, they could not fit the dead man into his pack, as his legs were too long. They cut off his legs at the knee and buried his remains in the damp earth of the bog but just as they were returning to their cottage, the corpse sat up and shouted out a chilling curse: -

> **'You think you laid me snug in clay**
> **But I shall rise in night or day**
> **And I'll haunt ye far and I'll haunt ye near**
> **Father and son with terror and fear**
> **Across the seas and every nation**
> **Right down to the nineteenth generation!'**

The curse came true and the next evening, the cottage door burst open and there was the body of the pedlar. He was covered in blood and he moved around on his stumps. He tortured the couple that night and every night after so that the wife's hair turned white and her husband became an old bent over man.

Even when they emigrated to America, 'Stumpie' as he became known as, followed the couple on the ship and to every place where they settled. He haunted them to their dying day.

There came each night a terrible slither,
A stumpie sound going hither and thither.

It is said that the Stumpie's prophecy about haunting the family down through the generations has happened and there are still some years to go. With regards to the area now known as Stumpie's Brae, there is a warning:

> **Ye'll ken it weel, through the few fir trees,**
> **The house where they wont to dwell;**
> **Gin ye meet ane there, as daylight flees,**
> **Stumping about on the banes o'his knees,**
> **It'll just be oul Stumpie himself' tae please!**

The Midnight Pact with Satan, East Co. Down

Long ago in East Down, a retired army colonel lived in a great house with his wife and family. He was well known for his penny-pinching ways and his love of all things gold. One Halloween night, when ghosts would begin their weary wander on earth, he decided to pray to the devil for more of the precious metal. After some time the room was filled with a putrid smell and when he looked up, he saw a young handsome, well-dressed man. However, on looking down, he noticed that the man had cloven feet! At the end of that bewitched Halloween night, a dreadful pact had been made and signed in blood by both parties.

The agreement was that for the next twenty-five years, the devil would agree to grant all the colonel's wishes but afterwards, the old man's body and soul would belong to him. Once agreed, the devil vanished. The colonel began to think that the whole episode was merely a bad dream and he doubted that the agreement had indeed taken place. As a test, he decided to summon the devil once again and ordered him to fill up a nearby house with gold. Promptly agreeing, the devil climbed onto the roof and through a hole, he shoveled thousands of gold coins into the house. He stopped for a while and looked into the house and saw that the colonel had made a hole in the floor and all the gold was going into the foundations. He was very angry that the colonel was hiding the gold so that the devil would have to fill the house with even more gold.

Confronting the colonel, the devil warned, *"Learn once and for all"* he roared. *"Although I'm your servant, I'm not to be trifled with"*. He then instantly disappeared.

Many years past and the colonel lived happily off his hoard of gold. However, he and his wife were on very bad terms and were always arguing with one another. After one particularly bad night of screaming at each other, the colonel decided on a final solution.

He summoned the devil once again and told him that he could no longer stand living with his wife. The devil knew what he had to do. One of the man's daughters was heard screaming upstairs and rushed down to tell her father that her mother had taken a violent seizure and was dying. Rushing upstairs, the man discovered that his wife had been strangled and lay dead on the bedroom floor. There were marks on her neck and her eyes bulged in terror.

The colonel was full of remorse when he realised what he had done and remained alone in his room for days on end, hardly eating. He even pleaded with the devil to return his wife back to life again but it was too late. The devil reminded him that he could not 'remove the stains from his soul'.

As the end of the twenty-five years came closer, the colonel realised that the devil would be returning to claim his soul. He broke out in a cold sweat at the thought of it and wondered if there was any way out of the pact that he had foolishly entered into all those years ago. After a lot of thought, he thought of a plan and summoned the devil once again and commanded that he produce something that had never been made before. The devil was curious,*"I want you to make me a rope of sand!"* the man laughed, thinking that he had outwitted the devil at last. If he could not make a rope of sand, then he could not claim the man's soul, as he not fully served him for twenty-five years.

The devil flew into a rage, shouting and swearing at the man and unbuckling his belt, he violently hit out at the man's face. The man felt an intense burning sensation in his eye as if hot sand had been poured into the socket. He cried in agony and realised that he was now blind in this eye. The devil laughed and disappeared again.

Halloween night was approaching fast and the colonel was in despair. He began to repent his evil ways and prayed to God for help. The fateful day arrived and the man was thin and pale with fear. Just as the day was finishing, the devil appeared ready to claim the doomed man's soul and asked if there were any final requests which he could grant. In desperation, the man thought of a plan and asked the devil to build him a brand new mill on his land and added that it must be finished that night.

After several hours, the devil performed his final deed and the man could see the brand new mill. All the local people flocked to see the brand new building and the man took refuge inside.

As midnight drew closer, the devil confronted the old man, *"Your time has come,"* he said. *"I have come to claim your soul!"* But as he went to grab him, the man held up the bible in front of him. The devil backed away. *"You cannot escape!"* mocked the devil. *"This is a journey we must both undertake!"* The colonel pleaded for his life and then cried out God's name as a last defence. The devil let out an unmerciful scream and suddenly vanished in a blaze of fire through a hole in the wall.

Satan's grip on the wretched old man was released at long last. For the rest of his life the old colonel remained a devout hermit and undertook penance for all his sins. He publicly declared his evil pact with Satan and what he had done and died peacefully a number of years later. The mill itself stood for many years and became known as the Devil's Mill and still remains today though it is in ruins. This mill, built by unearthly forces can still be recognised. On one of the cornerstones, five long black fingers are burnt permanently into the brickwork.

Hell's Fire is Your Lot, Leitrim, Co. Down

In the 1800s, there once existed a small hill farm in Leitrim that seemed to be cursed, as no crops would grow on it.

A young widow eventually purchased the farm with the intention of making a living out of it for her and her young child. Local people were puzzled by this, especially as she had little or no farming experience and she was often ridiculed as she passed by her neighbours.

The following spring was very wet and brought disaster to many farmers as their crops were destroyed and potatoes blighted. However, for some strange reason, all was well on the widow's farm with lush green grass and crops. One neighbouring farmer decided to visit the widow to congratulate her. He set out on a very wet summer's day but as he approached her cottage the sun was shining, yet when he looked back all he saw were dark clouds and skies.

No one appeared to be at home and as he was about to walk away, he overheard a voice. Looking through one of the windows, he caught sight of the young widow inside asking for many requests as she read from a large black book. He knocked on the door and was invited to enter inside. Asking for a drink of milk to distract the widow, he managed to look at the book, which was in another room. On the book's front cover was the words, 'READ ME ALL THROUGH BUT PRACTICE ME NOT, FOR IF YOU DO HELL'S FIRE IS YOUR LOT'.

He quickly returned to the front room to wait for his milk and looked through a small crack in a door at his host who was in the scullery. She had stuck a fork into a table and milk was pouring out of the holes and into a glass. On observing this strange sight, the farmer quickly left the cottage and hurried straight to the parish priest to relate his story.

A few hours later, the priest decided to call at the widow's home for himself. Just as he was half way up the lane, his horse went crazy and he fell off. Shaking and bruised, the priest continued on his way to the cottage on foot. The door opened as he came nearer and he could see the widow inside shouting, *"Leave this house! Leave this house!"*

The priest held firm and implored the young widow to destroy the book and never to read from it again.

Immediately, the front door slammed shut and the cottage burst into flames! Helpless, the priest watched as it was completely destroyed. All the lush green grass turned to rushes and it started to rain once again on the farm. Neighbours rushed to the farm when they saw the flames but there was no sign of the bodies of the widow or her child. All that remained was the large black book and it remained intact and undamaged by the fire.

One neighbour carefully wrapped the book in a cloth and buried it under an old oak tree, where, to this day, it remains buried and not to be disturbed.

The mystery of the hill farm and the book has never been explained. Some say that the widow had been once visited by a man dressed in black. He promised her a good life as long as he could have her soul in return. Who was this mysterious man? Some say it was the Devil himself!

Galgorm Castle, Ballymena, Co. Antrim

The building is a fine example of Jacobean architecture dating from 1618 and was originally the estate of Rory Og McQuillan before being taken over by Sir Faithful Fortescue who built the existing castle. He was hated by the local people so much so that they tried to burn down the castle.

The castle was sold to a Doctor Alexander Colville and it is believed that he was involved in black magic and had actually sold his soul to the devil in return for money and knowledge. One story is that in exchange of his soul, the devil promised Colville enough gold to fill his boot. By making a hole in the floorboards and the boot, which he nailed down, Colville tried to outwit and cheat the devil. It took the demons several journeys to fill the boot to the top but little did they realise that the gold was accumulating beneath the floor.

Galgorm Castle, Ballymena

After Dr. Colville died, the devil punished him by making his soul wander through the castle for all time and it is said that his footsteps can be heard as he does his rounds throughout the night. Other nights, a ghostly light is seen around the park as he searches for his long lost gold. It is also said that his portrait must never be removed from the castle and anyone who touches it will be doomed!

The castle now overlooks the tenth green of the local golf course and recently became a filming location for 'The Frankenstein Chronicles'.

Hawkin's Ghost, Rathfriland, Co. Down

Squire Hawkins, whose grave lies in the Drumballyroney Church graveyards, was reputedly one of the founder members of the Rathfriland Hell-Fire Club. The Hell-Fire Club was one of a number throughout Ireland and England during the 18th and 19th centuries. Its members were often misguided men or 'rakes' of that time who were only interested in partying, immoral activities, debauchery, the Black Art and also devil worship. There is no evidence of any such devil worship in the Rathfriland branch where they held their meetings in the cellar of the former Clanwilliam Arms in the Square.

When the wealthy Hawkins died, his coffin was carried on the back of a horse-drawn carriage from Rathfriland to Ballyroney with his family and servants walking behind. On reaching the gates of the churchyard, the black horses reared up and foamed at the mouth. Despite the efforts of the servants, the horses refused to enter into the graveyard. They were whipped and pulled back and forward, this way and that but nothing could get them to go through the gates. Eventually, the Squire's coffin had to be lifted from the hearse and carried through the gates to his grave where it was lowered and covered over with soil.

Later that night, while everyone was sleeping soundly they were awakened by one of the most ferocious storms to hit the town of Rathfriland. Some people said that this was the noise of the devil as he came to claim the Squire's soul for himself! The next day some family members came to check on Squire Hawkins grave. They could not believe their eyes.

Sometime, during the thunderstorm of the previous night, the family tombstone had been struck by lightning and there was the sign of the cross formed on the stone. Everyone was convinced that this was God's way of getting his revenge on the Squire, as he had not believed in his existence during his life. This cross was a warning it was said from God himself not to dabble with the forces of darkness.

Hawkins Grave, Drumballyroney Co. Down

Hill' when all of a sudden he heard what sounded like footsteps behind him. He assumed that these were coming from another traveller who was also making his way home. The footsteps got louder and louder until they sounded more like hooves as if someone was approaching on horseback. The man turned around, expecting to see a horse and its rider but what he actually saw was a more monstrous figure.

It was the hideous spectre of the figure of a man with horns on his head, the face of a ghost and instead of feet it had cloven hooves: it was the Devil himself! The man was so frightened that he started to run for his life and said the Lord's Prayer as he did so. Ever after that incident, he refused to walk home again alone and he never returned to the Hell-Fire Club.

The Devil and the Gamblers, Co. Derry

There are many stories of people who have claimed to have encountered the devil himself while playing cards. The following tale comes from the City of Derry in the early 1900s.

The same group of men used to meet regularly to have a game of cards. One night they were having a drink in a pub near Bishop Street when they invited a stranger to play cards with them. When he started to lose large sums of money, they were happy to meet up again with him for more games. They would all meet at an old blacksmith's forge at the top of Howard Street. Gradually the stranger started to win back his money and the men were becoming very angry when they started to lose theirs including their weekly wages.

One night, in desperation, a member of the group remarked that he would sell his soul to beat the newcomer. At this, the newcomer laughed and thumped the table. When the dealer bent down to pick up the scattered cards, he noticed that the newcomer had cloven feet. He decided to run away and urged his friends to do the same, however the man who made the remark about selling his soul, froze in fear and could not move. His friends tried to drag him away but the stranger was also holding on to him. Eventually, they managed to free their friend and they all ran quickly away from the scene, not stopping until they had reached St. Columb's Well.

From the streetlights, they saw the imprint of the devil's fingers burnt into their friend's arm. They all quickly blessed themselves and at that moment in time, they saw the flames lick into the night sky. The next morning they also heard that their meeting place, the blacksmith's forge, had been burnt to the ground.

A Dance with the Devil, Hilltown, Co. Down

During the 1970s, a group of young girls travelled from Rostrevor to a dance in Hilltown. It was the 'in' place at the time for ceilidhs, country and western dances and many young people travelled there from far and wide. Boys and girls would attend in the hope of finding a new partner and because there were people from all over the country, there were lots of new faces each night.

One of the Rostrevor girls spotted this handsome young fella from across the dance floor and she admitted to her friends that she would love to dance with him. He was tall, cleanly shaven and had long brown hair. The others spitefully remarked that she would stand no chance and he was unlikely to look twice at her. However, she noticed him looking around the hall and his eyes met hers and he stared at her for a while before smiling back. Moments later, he moved towards the girl and taking her hand he asked her for a dance. Her friends could not believe her luck as he was the best looking man there. The couple never left the dance floor all night and were getting on a like a house on fire. The girl was starting to think that she had met her future husband.

Eventually, the music stopped at one o'clock and the couple left the hall together. They decided to go to the local 'chippy' at the bottom of the street for some food before they went home. As they walked hand in hand down the street, the girl glanced down at her companion's feet and realised that he was not wearing any shoes and in fact he had hoofed or clubbed feet.

Terrified, she ran off as fast as she could to get away from him. She had realised that the man of her dreams was in fact the 'devil' himself. Her screams could be heard all over Hilltown. Her friends had seen her panic and were able to describe how the young man simply disappeared before their very eyes and could not be found anywhere. Their friend was traumatised for a long time after that encounter.

Chapter 11
Poltergeist Stories

The word poltergeist is German and means 'boisterous ghost'. The ghost is invisible but makes all sorts of strange noises and even moves objects around a room. The haunting is usually linked with a certain individual and therefore differs from other ghosts. There are a number of unexplained such stories throughout Ulster.

The Cooneen Poltergeist, Co. Fermanagh

One of the most famous and strangest poltergeist stories comes from Co. Fermanagh in the townland of Cornarooslan, Cooneen near the Tyrone border. Cooneen is derived from 'An Cúinnín' meaning the 'little corner'. The story was reported widely in the local newspapers and some Hollywood movies are actually based on it.

Back in 1914, the widow Murphy was living here with her seven children in an isolated cottage. One night they heard strange noises coming from the loft followed by strange knocks and scraping. On investigation, nothing could be seen. Eventually, whatever was causing the disturbances became much more aggressive and began throwing pots around the room and would close drawers on the children's fingers.

Deserted House at Cooneen, Co. Fermanagh (Courtesy of G.S.I.)

Local priests came to investigate and support the family. They witnessed a number of strange and unexplained events over many visits. One such chilling experience was in one of the bedrooms where they witnessed bedclothes rising and falling on an empty bed as if someone was underneath breathing. Strange noises were also heard emanating from the spirit including snoring and then followed by spitting and hissing. When questions were asked in English, Latin or Irish, they were all answered correctly. When one of the priests sprinkled holy water around a room, the poltergeist went crazy, making very loud knocks and bangs as it ran around the walls.

Some people suggested that it was all a hoax caused by the children. Tests were carried out so that the children were unable to move their arms or feet but the knocking continued so much so that the men, who were holding the children, fled from the room terrified. No exorcism was ever carried out as in the end Mrs. Murphy decided to leave the cottage and emigrate to America. There was no further appearance of the poltergeist after that. However, some people have said that the spirit followed the family while they crossed the Atlantic. A number of passengers on the ship complained of rapping's and bangs coming from the Murphy's cabin and captain actually warned Mrs. Murphy that the noises would have to stop or else they would be put off the ship.

It is known that the poltergeist even followed the family to their new home in America but eventually the disturbances subsided and the family was able to live their lives in peace. The priests who had investigated the case all suffered badly from their experiences, one had a nervous breakdown, another developed spinal meningitis and a third priest suffered from facial paralysis.

The Drumfanad Ghost, Co. Donegal

Drumfanad is located on the Fanad peninsula lying between Lough Swilly and Mulroy Bay in North Donegal. The name is derived from 'Droim Fada' meaning 'the long ridge'.

This story is from the late 18th Century and was first recorded in the 'London-Derry Journal' on November 7th, 1786 when a letter from Ramelton described unsuccessful attempts to exorcise a ghost. Further versions of the same story have been told over the years since.

Apparently, this ghost had caused the windows of the house to rattle, even on a quiet day. The delph would fall from the dresser and smash into pieces on the stone floor and various items of furniture would move around the rooms on their own. It is also claimed that the disturbances even continued outside when the cattle would charge wildly around the field, cows would miscarry and the milk would not churn. This went on for several years until drastic action was needed.

It took at least three people to exorcise the evil spirit. Some stories state that it was three clergymen while another story involves freemasons who came from Letterkenny. The first record in 1786 stated that when the clergymen started praying, a violent noise was heard from a room upstairs sounding 'as if a thousand cats and dogs were joined together in horrid concert in opposition to the Reverend Gentlemen below'. An unknown hand started to play with their hats and wigs and their books were covered with turf mound. The clergymen had to leave the house when a shower of bricks and more turf was thrown at them.

Another story tells how the freemasons arrived with three cocks, a white, a red and a black cock. The house was cleared and the black cock was thrown in and the door shut. They heard the cock squawking and scurrying around inside and then silence. When they opened the door, the cock was lying on the floor, dead. They next threw in the red cock and the same thing happened only it survived with a broken wing. When the white cock was thrown in, the windows were blown out, the roof rose and slates flew off. Inside the furniture was thrown about and the delph was smashed. Eventually, the ghostly figure was seen leaving through the chimney. It howled as it travelled across the sky before disappearing into a hole in a nearby field where it has remained ever since.

Meanwhile, the freemasons continued to read from their Holy Writ and on opening the front door, they saw that the house was wrecked inside while the white cock strutted outside completely unscathed.

Some people argued that the trouble in the house only happened when one particular servant girl was present. To this day a white cock has always been kept at this farm.

The Trinity Street Ghost, Belfast

The Rushlight Magazine in Belfast tells the story of the Trinity Street Ghost. Trinity Street is beside Clifton Street just off the Westlink in North Belfast. In 1931, a new family moved in and also rented out rooms to other tenants. Soon afterwards strange things started to happen, doors and windows opened and banged shut on their own and many of the tenants claimed to have heard strange noises from the outside coal shed. Others said they had seen a 'young man surrounded by a bright light' in different parts of the house. Some of the tenants tied their room doors closed at night but would find the cord broken the next morning.

Before long crowds of onlookers would stand outside the house to catch a glimpse of the strange being. Even a medium was called to ask the being to leave. The story reached the local and national newspapers and the police were called to control the crowd outside the house.

Many theories were put forward for the strange happenings including one story that a young man had been murdered in the house and his body was buried under the shed. However, the landlord refused to all any excavation work to be carried out.

After some time, the tenants had had enough and decided to leave the dwelling and the sightings and noises suddenly ceased even when a new family moved in.

No one has been able to explain the Trinity Street Ghost but it was a great story recalled by many over the years.

The Larne Poltergeist, Co. Antrim

A mid 19th Century story appeared in the Larne Reporter of 1866. It concerned two families who resided near Larne. Both houses were subject to stones being thrown at them throughout the day and night. The story spread out and many people turned up to observe this strange event. On another occasion, a bag of potatoes was emptied into the kitchen where a number of neighbours had gathered.

It was believed that many years previously a nearby farmer was tortured by mischievous fairies and was forced to leave his cottage, which fell into disrepair. His story became forgotten and the stones of his cottage were used to repair their neighbour's dwellings. This angered the fairies once again and they manifested their anger by the incidents mentioned.

The Derrygonnelly Farmhouse Ghost, Co. Fermanagh

This was a famous 19th Century haunting as it was investigated by Sir William Barrett, a former President of the Society for Psychic Research.

The story centres involved a widower who lived in a small farmhouse with his son and four daughters. His eldest daughter was called Maggie and it is said that the haunting centred on her after her mother had died.

It all started one night with loud banging and scratching sounds heard throughout the house. This got worse over time when objects were moved around and even found outside. The father was advised to leave an open Bible in the house and to weigh down its pages with some stones. However, in the morning, the stones had been removed and some of the pages had even been ripped out of the book.

Sir William Barrett and several others observed the happenings in the house for themselves. When all the children had gone to bed, he heard noises coming from the walls, the ceiling and the bedroom where Maggie was lying fully clothed on her bed. They entered the room with a lamp and the noises stopped but started up again when the lamp was placed on a windowsill. They were unable to identify the source of the noises. As they watched Maggie, a pebble suddenly appeared on the bed beside her.

The investigators visited the house for several nights and the same events occurred each time. Barrett even asked the source of the noises how many fingers he was showing in his pockets and the correct answers were given by the number of raps.

In the end, one of the ministers who was with Barrett, read out loud some passages from the Bible. The noises started to diminish and eventually stopped altogether after he recited the Lord's Prayer. The Haunting had come to an end!

Strange Happenings in Articlave, Co. Derry

This story was reported in the 1930s and involved a farmer and his family who were tortured by strange noises and events in their small farmhouse.

Household items were hurled around the kitchen including a lamp, which had been sitting on the table. Although there was no one near it, it was suddenly raised and hurled against the ceiling breaking its globe. A tin of paint was also thrown from the scullery against the kitchen wall and clothes were slashed. But worse of all their young daughter was also being victimised.

When they put her to sleep, she was jagged by pins and nipped in her arm until it was black and blue. Her father was worried about his daughter and was considering sending her away to relatives for her own safety. Anyone else who slept in her bed also suffered the same treatment. Some neighbours even witnessed the events.

Eventually, the farmer reported the matter to the police. He was able to say that the strange events started about six months previously and coincided with the burning of hay and straw in the fields. It was claimed that one police constable had been left alone in the kitchen to keep watch. He suddenly heard a voice coming out of the shadows, "*There is only you and me*", it said. Immediately, the constable grabbed his boots and replied, "*Wait until I get my boots on and there will only be you!*"

Eventually, the occurrences started to get fewer and fewer. The family were relieved and hopeful that they would stop completely. No explanation could ever be found!

Mysterious Happenings at Magilligan. Co. Derry

Supernatural manifestations were reported in 1907, at a farmhouse near Magilligan belonging to John and Sophia McLaughlin, and elderly brother and sister who lived in a small one-storey farmhouse.

As was normal practice at that time, John had cleaned the kitchen chimney with the branches of a holly bush and buried the soot outside. But soon afterwards, the couple were plagued by soot so that cooking became impossible and cakes of soot were thrown around the kitchen marking the walls and breaking the delph. Stones also appeared and were thrown against the windows of the house breaking the panes from the inside. Noises were also heard at night but all the damage was done during the day. Once again no explanation could be given for the strange happenings which eventually stopped themselves.

Mysterious Noises near Bridge End Railway Station, Inishowen, Co. Donegal

In the 1940s, Patrick Canning lived in Aileach Beg, a townland on the eastern shores of Lough Swilly. He had purchased the house and had lived there quite contentedly for a number of years. However, after the death of the previous owner of the house, strange things started to occur.

The former owner was very attached to the property and found it hard to leave but as he was unable to look after himself and the farm, the family sold it on. After he died, the Canning family started to hear loud raps on the outside doors both back and front and windows started to rattle. They also heard the sound of chains being dragged in the yard outside. The noises continued until four in the morning.

Inishowen Peninsula, Co. Donegal

The story spread through the neighbourhood and several neighbours agreed to keep watch to make sure that this was not of the work of a prankster. However, they also heard the same noises and could not understand who or what was responsible.

Eventually, a local priest was called in and after that the noises were not heard again. All agreed that it was the spirit of the former owner whose spirit was not at rest.

Chapter 12
Ancient Myths & Legends

Ulster, like the rest of Ireland is a land steeped in myth and mystery, a land rich in stories and tales told by our ancestors. Many of our ancient structures, dolmens and graves feature strongly in Irish myths. The collection below is only some of the more ancient tales that exist.

The Last Serpent of Ireland-Lig na Paiste, Co. Derry

The Sperrin Mountains divide the County of Derry and one of its rivers, the Owenreagh, rises in the Parish of Banagher and flows northeast through a deep wooded glen.

Back in the 6th Century, shortly after the death of St. Patrick, the local people here were still being terrorised by a great serpent, a giant fire breathing dragon. They could not understand why this particular serpent was missed by St. Patrick when he banished all the others from the entire island of Ireland.

The serpent had laid waste to the land from the slopes of the Sperrin Mountains to the shores of Lough Foyle. It became known as 'Lig na Paiste', which means 'the last of the serpents'.

The local people were desperate and pleaded with a local holy man, Saint Murrough O'Heaney for help in getting rid of the evil serpent. Murrough had a church in the glen – Banagher Old Church. Its ruins and St. Murrough's grave can still be seen today. St. Murrough agreed to help the people and fasted for ten days and ten nights praying for guidance and knowledge to defeat the serpent.

With his newfound strength, St. Murrough went straight to the place where the serpent had his lair, a deep pool in the nearby river. He had three rods made from the reeds of the river with him. He enticed the serpent out of the river. The serpent had initially thought the man standing before it was just another sacrifice from the locals so it was not suspicious. St. Murrough managed to place the rods on the serpent and then called upon God to change the rods to steel. Immediately, the serpent was encased in a steel cage, unable to escape.

Below is the sculpture of Lis na Paiste by Maurice Harron, Feeny, Co. Derry

The serpent started to beg for forgiveness but St. Murrough held firm and told the serpent would be forever encased in steel at the bottom of Lough Foyle, never to rise again. The serpent asked then to be able to look upon Ciannact from its watery prison and St. Murrough agreed to that request. Ciannact is the area that stretches from Banagher and the Sperrins to Lough Foyle.

Some people still say that Lig na Paiste coils and writhes under the waters of Lough Foyle in a vain attempt to free itself from its cage of steel. This accounts for the unusual currents and high tides in the Lough.

Lough Shannagh Monster, Co. Down

W. D. Fitzpatrick tells the story of the most terrible water dragon ever known in Ireland which set up home in Lough Shannagh deep in the Mourne Mountains of County Down.

It would devour at least fifty cattle each day and if the local people did not provide this daily food, the monster would hunt down and kill every human being it could find. Its presence was causing devastation among the population and all the farms for miles around. One of the local chieftains was called Aidan and he and some of his men were summoned to deal with the monster and to force it to depart. One of Aidan's advisors Ablach volunteered to approach the dragon and find out why it had come to the Mournes and what it would take to get rid of it. As Ablach and his comrades approached the lake, the beast emerged and raised its head from the water letting out a terrible roar.

Ablach understood that the dragon was demanding sixty steeds by sunrise otherwise it would devour all. The Chieftain ordered Ablach to tell the dragon that this wish was impossible and no one was scared of the dragon anymore. As Ablach relayed the message, he stepped back from the dragon so that he would be a safe distance from its ferocious jaws. However, the dragon was so angry at what he had been told that he opened his huge jaws and with a roaring intake of breath, it sucked Alblach down its throat. It then rolled out of the lake, as it had no limbs and attacked the rest of Aidan's men swallowing them whole.

The chieftain Aidan was enraged by this and raced to the dragon himself throwing himself onto the monster's neck. With all his strength, he twisted and twisted its neck round and round until it was forced to roll over on its back. The monster was then unable to get up. Aidan held firm while his remaining men rushed to the scene and cut open the monsters throat.

Out spilled Ablach and the other warriors the dragon had devoured. They all looked well despite their ordeal. After this, the monster was let go and it slid back into the lake where it sank to the bottom like a massive stone. Everyone in the Mournes was overjoyed when they heard that the dragon had been slain. They lit bonfires on all the peaks and celebrated for nine days and nights. Chieftain Aidan and his men were honoured as heroes.

Finn McCool Legends

Finn McCool (Fionn Mac Cumhaill) was a well-known warrior/ giant. Legend has it that Finn once had a long and fierce battle with another giant from the other edge of Carlingford Lough. Finn was situated in the Slieve Foy side while the other giant was now standing on the County Down side. They fought long and hard and while Finn was sleeping, the other giant sneaked over the water and stole Finn's sword. When Finn awoke, he fell in to a great rage and started to throw stones and boulders across the lough.

One stone was the Cloughmore Stone which weighed over fifty tons. With all his strength, Finn managed to throw it across the lough at the other giant. It landed on the unfortunate's head, crushing his great body into the mountain where it melted away like snow beneath the stone.

The Cloughmore Stone still lies above Rostrevor village. It is said that it and other rocks on Slieve Meen originated in the Cooley Mountains which lie on the other side of the lough and vice versa. Walking around the Cloughmore Stone seven times will allegedly bring good luck.

While climbing Slieve Gullion in Co. Armagh, Finn came across a beautiful maiden who was weeping at the edge of the lake on top of the mountain. She told him she had dropped her gold ring into the lake and was unable to retrieve it herself as it was said to be bottomless. Finn duly obliged however and dived into the lake. After some time, he managed to locate the ring and bring it to the maiden but she had turned into an old hag 'the Calliagh Berra' and was laughing at him. She then turned him into an old withered man. When he made his way back down the mountain, no one recognised him apart from his trusty old hounds.

With his men, the Fianna and the hounds the Calliagh Berra was forced to reverse her spell on Finn and restore him to his youth once again. However, it is said that his hair remained white for the rest of his days.

His fate may also befall anyone who bathes in the lake to this day!

Another legend associated with Finn lies in Seafin Castle (Sidhe Finn meaning 'the Seat of Finn McCool'). It is situated alongside the River Bann in Drumballyroney, in Co. Down. It is claimed that Finn and his soldiers often stayed there to rest between their many battles.

The remains of Seafin Castle, Co. Down

One particular story describes how Finn brought a beautiful young lady back to the Castle after one such battle. She had put a spell on Finn and he was completely under her power. His warriors, however, noticed that she took on the appearance of an old witch while she slept. They decided to get rid of her and threw her body in the nearby River Bann. The river bubbled and turned red and black as she disappeared under the water. Some say her reflection can still be seen if one looks closely into the water near the ruined castle.

The Ardboe Cow, Co. Tyrone

Ardboe lies on the shores of Lough Neagh and was the site of a 6th Century monastery founded by St. Colman. It still has a 10th Century High Cross in the area. It is claimed that many hundreds of years ago, while the monastery was being built at Ardboe, the lough ran dry and there was no water to make any more mortar. The monks prayed for rain but rather than water, a cow arose from the bottom of the lough. Its milk was then used to mix the mortar. This legend is preserved in the name Ardboe where 'Ard Bó' means 'the height of the cow'.

Saint Bronach's Bell, Rostrevor, Co. Down

Many hundreds of years ago, County Down was ruled by the local chieftains. One such chieftain was Fergus of Glenn Secis. One day he was out hunting red deer in the Mourne Mountains near the Deer's Meadow. He and his men came across a mighty stag, which he resolved to capture with the help of his two favourite hounds. Fergus ventured out on his own to accomplish this task and when he caught up with the stag, he was surprised to see a rival chieftain, Artan of Lecale also pursuing the same deer.

As the dogs attacked the stag, one of Artan's hounds was gored to death by its sharp antlers. Artan was dismayed and annoyed on losing his best hound and he fired his javelin at the stag but instead killed the hound of Fergus. This in turn enraged Fergus and thinking Artan's act was done deliberately, he shot an arrow at Artan hitting him on the chest.

Grief stricken, Fergus carried his dead hound home. As time passed by, he started to become nervous and irritable and feared a war would evolve between his and Artan's Clan. Fergus became very religious and commissioned a bell and twelve bronze candlesticks and presented them to Saint Bronach and her religious community in Rostrevor. Bronach placed the bell in a recess in an oak tree near her church.

Fergus still was not happy and decided to leave his chieftaincy and as a further act of atonement, he dressed himself in sackcloth and sandals and left the area completely to travel as a pilgrim through many lands far away. After almost fifty years of penance, he decided to return home.

On his return he found his homeland ravaged by the Danes and the convent and church in ruins. He came across an old man near the church and he enquired what had happened. During the conversation Fergus realised that he was actually talking to Artan of Lecale who he had thought he had killed all those many years ago.

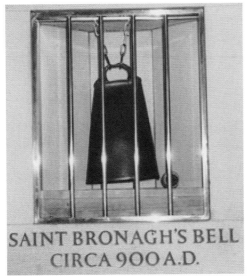

SAINT BRONAGH'S BELL
CIRCA 900 A.D.

Artan explained that he had only been injured but even though he lay ill for many weeks, he survived. Fergus's heart swelled with gratitude and the weight of his life burden was lifted off him. Suddenly, a breeze shook the trees and the old bell rang out. Fergus started to tremble and he fell on his knees begging Artan to forgive him. Fergus then fell forward and died in the arms of his old enemy.

For the next thousand years, the bell was heard ringing but its source could never be found. It was said that when the bell rang in the morning it was for joy. Before a storm, the bell warned of the coming danger and before a death it is said that the banshee tolled the bell. If the bell rang at a funeral there was the promise of rest and immortality for the departed soul.

After many centuries the bell suddenly stopped ringing and no one could explain its absence. Future generations became sceptical of the bell's history and the stories attached to it. In 1885, a large oak which stood beside the old church in Kilbroney Cemetery was blown down during a bad storm.

Afterwards workmen started to saw up the old tree. Suddenly, they discovered a recess in the trunk and inside was the 'ghostly bell'.

They also found the bell's tongue at the bottom of the recess and this explained why the bell was not heard as it had lost its ability to create a sound.

Saint Bronach's Bell is now located in the Catholic Church in Rostrevor.

Ossian's Grave, Cushendall, Co. Antrim

This is a megalithic court cairn situated on the Cushendall to Ballymoney Road. It is said that it contains the grave of Ossian (or Oisín), a Celtic warrior poet and son of Finn McCool. He waits here for the right moment at which to rise from his grave.

Recently, a young couple visited the site and it was here that the man proposed to his girlfriend. Suddenly, they both heard a terrifying scream which caused their ears to ring for hours afterwards. Was this Ossian warning them to move away from his grave?

Annaghmare Court Tomb, Co. Armagh

Annaghmare Tomb is situated west of Slieve Gullion and is a fine example of that type of structure. 'Ath na Marbh' means 'the ford of the dead'.

It is also known as the Black Castle and is said to be the home of a number of ghostly apparitions. It was excavated in the 1960s and archaeologists found the remains of human bones, some pottery and flint and also bear teeth.

Chapter 13
Other Mysteries & Unusual Stories

The Haunted Gates of Finnebrogue, Co. Down

Finnebrogue House is a 17th Century mansion and it is said to be the oldest inhabited dwelling in Northern Ireland. It lies near the banks of the Quoile River and Strangford Lough and is close to the ruins of the 12th Century Inch Abbey. It is said that the stones from the Abbey were used when building the entrance pillars.

Finnebrogue Gates, Co. Down

When workmen hung the huge ornamental gates, the next day the gates would be found laying flat on the ground yet the gates brackets remained untouched. Each time the gates were hung, they were found on the ground the following day.

It was decided to post men at the gates in order to unravel the mystery. The men waited patiently as darkness fell and then all of a sudden, they saw the gates lifting all by themselves and falling on the ground nearby. There was no sign of anyone nearby. The men were clearly frightened and ran off to the house. Even without the gates, horses refused to pass through the pillars and they had to be dragged through them blindfolded. Many visitors had to dismount or leave their coaches and walk to the house.

Eventually, new pillars were built at a new entrance and driveway and the gates could be hung undisturbed. The haunted pillars of Finnebrogue became overgrown and remain so to this day. No explanation has ever been given for this strange story.

Lurgan Woman Buried Twice, Co. Armagh

The fear of being buried alive is a real one and became a reality for a young Lurgan woman called Marjorie McCall back in 1705. In those days, graves were often dug up so that the robbers would remove any valuables such as jewellery from the bodies.

Her husband was a type of surgeon and after she became ill and then unconscious, her family was satisfied that she was dead. At her wake, many tried to remove a valuable ring, which she always wore but it could not be removed. Anyway, she was buried in Shankhill Graveyard and that very night her body was exhumed by robbers who were after her ring.

They also could not remove the ring and decided to cut off her finger. As soon as blood was drawn from poor Marjorie, she woke from her coma. The robbers were so frightened that they ran from the graveyard and never looked back. Marjorie managed to climb out of the grave and made her way home.

Her family was all gathered around the fire at her house to keep her husband company after his sad loss. Marjorie knocked at the door. Her husband declared, *"If your mother was still alive, I'd swear that was her knock"*. And sure enough, when he opened the door, he saw his wife, dressed in her burial clothes and very much alive. He then fainted on the spot.

It is reported that Marjorie lived for some years after this event and when she did die, she was buried once again in Shankill Graveyard. Her gravestone exists today and bears the inscription '**Lived Once, Buried Twice**'.

Headstone of Majorie McCaul, Lurgan, Co. Armagh

Belvoir Park Hospital, Belfast

Belvoir Park is a large expanse of woodland situated in south Belfast; it also contains the former Belvoir Park Hospital. It was the former Purdysburn Fever Hospital from the 1900s and then the main centre for radiotherapy treatment for N. Ireland before it closed in 2006. Since then, it has been guarded by security and strange stories then came out of the hospital. Guards would see shadowy figures running through the site. Then shrines were discovered by edge of the stream which flows nearby as well as a number of mutilated corpses.

The Mysterious Lady in Blue, Buncrana, Co. Donegal

Some years ago, a young girl went missing in the Buncrana area. Her family were distraught especially her older sister who was supposed to have kept an eye on her. The sister was helping in the search and was very relieved when she saw a local man walking towards her holding the hand of her younger sister. He explained that when he had been near the sea wall, he saw a lady dressed in a long blue dress leading the little girl out of the water. She told him to take the child back to her family and for them to ensure that she must always be safe near water. The man looked back after a while but there was no sign of the lady.

Some years later, that same young girl became a nun and was working in Naples in Italy as a nursing tutor in the local hospital. Along with another nun from Derry, she went swimming in the Bay of Naples. Although she was a strong swimmer by now, she was dragged out to sea and when rescued by local fishermen, she had unfortunately drowned.

Her family back home in Ireland was given the sad news. They then remembered her childhood experience and the warning given by the lady in blue. They often wonder if this was an omen for the future.

Unsettled Corpse, Creeve, Pomeroy, Co. Tyrone

This story came from 1750 from the small townland of Creeve and was described in the publication 'Ghostly Tales from Local Folklore'. Creeve is derived form 'craobh' meaning a 'wide spreading tree'.

Creeve was occupied by a number of local families who leased their properties from the Trench family. Down through the years, the family buried their dead in their own private graveyard.

One particular family member died and although he had expressed a wish to be buried with his fathers, his family ignored it and buried him in a local cemetery. For a week, nothing unusual occurred but then the family's cattle began to fall ill and the family members could not sleep at night. This continued until, in despair, they told the local priest about their plight. He advised them to rebury their relative's body in the family burial ground and all would be well. They followed his instructions and the cattle improved at once and the family were able to get some sleep. Their deceased relative was now at rest!

The Vanishing Village of Audley's Town, Co. Down

Audley's Town was part of the Castleward Estate and held over twenty-five families. Following the death of Viscount Bangor of Castleward, his widow Lady Harriet remarried and her new husband, Major Andrew Savage Nugent made a number of changes to the estate which were not well accepted. He disliked the poor inhabitants of Audley's Town and along with his new wife decided that replacing the village with new woodland would be more beneficial. The appearance of their dwellings was considered an eyesore and were ruining the views of Strangford Lough for the then 'lord and lady' of the manor.

Over one hundred and sixty years ago, all the villagers were apparently put on a boat to America and the village demolished. Little is left as a reminder of the village apart from some stone remains.

What became of the evicted tenants has become a bit of a mystery. After they sailed out of Strangford to Boston on board 'The Rose', they were never heard from again. Passengers with the surnames

of Hinds, Smyth and O'Connor were on board. Questions have
been asked - did they sail into another port? and more sinisterly;
did the captain get rid of his human cargo once he sailed out of the
lough?

Castle Ward itself is now managed by the National Trust and has
provided a filming location for the Game of Thrones series as well
as the Universal Movie - 'Dracula Untold'.

During the filming of Game of Thrones, the 16th Century
Tower and courtyards where used as the ancestral home of the
Stark family. Its grounds provided the setting for the Lannister
encampment in Series 1, the Baelor Battle and the Whispering
Wood. Visitors to Castle Ward can recreate the scene where Jon
Snow and Robb Stark teach Bran the art of archery. A recent Trail
includes Audley's Field and the castle. Audley's Field was used for
the filming of the aftermath of the battle of Oxcross when Robb
Stark meets his future wife Talisa.

The Cracked Tombstone in Newtownbreda Churchyard, Co. Down

Newtownbreda is a residential suburb of South East Belfast but
was once an 18th Century village.

Many years ago, a local man swore, for whatever reason, that when
he died that he would never lie quiet! When he passed away he was
buried and a stone placed over his grave but within a very short
period of time, the stone cracked. His wife was determined to buy
the heaviest tombstone she could afford and lay it over her 'restless'
husband. But the ghost was true to his word and the second stone
was once again broken in an effort to escape from his grave. Even
the third and heaviest stone was also cracked. It can still be seen in
the graveyard.

Bibliography

Names of Publications used

Banshees, Beasts and Brides from the Sea. Irish Tales of the Supernatural. Bob Curran. 2004. Appletree Press.

Ghostly Tales from Local Folklore, Vol 1. No. 1. Published by Park & Shields. 2000. (Irish Memories).

Haunted Belfast, Joe Baker. Nonsuch Publishing, Dublin. 2009.

Haunted Ireland. John J. Dunne. Appletree Press. 1989.

Haunted Ireland. Tarquin Blake. The Collins Press. 2014.

Irish Ghosts. A Ghost Hunter's Guide by Peter Amberly. 2012.

Irish Ghosts – Geddes and Grosset. 2010.

Irish Ghost Stories. Padraic O'Farrell. Gill Mac Millan.

Irish Ghost Stories & Mysteries from County Down. Annaclone Historical Society. 2014.

Journal of the Upper Ards Historical Society. No. 20 (1996) pp 29-32.

Ken McCormack's Derry. Heroes, Villains Ghosts. Ken McCormack. 2010. Colour Books, Dublin

Northern Ireland's Most Haunted Places. Lily Rooney

The Unexplained in Co. Down. Ghosts, Legends, Myths & Folklore. Annaclone Historical Society. 2011

True Irish Ghost Stories. John Seymour and Harry Neligan. Senate Press.1926.

Journals

Ulster Ghosts by W. Moore. The Irish Monthly. Vol. 57, No. 675. (September 1929).

Ulster Journal of Archaeology. Vol 17. No. 1 / 4. Feb-Nov 1911.

Webpages

www.belfasthistory.rushlightmagazine.com
www.creeslough.com
www.derryghosts.com
www.derryjournal.com
www.discoverloughneagh.com
www.donegaldaily.com
www.duchas.ie
www.galgormcastle.com
www.haunted-discoveries.co.uk
www.hauntedrooms.co.uk
www.hiddendublinwalks.com
www.ringofgullion.org
www.rushlightmagazine.com
www.st.johnstone and corrigans.com
www.spookyisles.com
www.theshadowlands.net/places/ireland

Facebook Pages

Haunted History
Ghost Searchers Ireland
Northernfrights

Newspapers and Magazines

The Ballymena Observer
The Derry Journal
The Dublin Daily Express
The Londonderry Sentinel
The Mid-Ulster Mail
The News Letter
Ulster Gazette.
Weekly Irish Times

Glossary

Placenames

Ulster is one of the four Provinces of Ireland, the others being Leinster, Munster and Connaught. The name 'Ulster' is derived from 'Cúige Ulaidh' named after the ancient people who lived in this part of Ireland.

The nine counties of Ulster are:-

Antrim – derived from 'Aontroim' meaning 'lone ridge';

Armagh – derived from 'Ard Macha' meaning 'Macha's Height';

Cavan – derived from 'an Cabhán' meaning 'the hollow';

Derry – derived from 'Doire' meaning 'Oak grove'.

Donegal – derived from 'Dún na nGall' meaning 'fort of the foreigners';

Down – derived from 'An Dún' meaning 'the fort';

Fermanagh – derived from 'Fir Manach' meaning 'men of Manach';

Monaghan – derived from 'Muineachán' meaning 'thickly overgrown area or hills';

Tyrone – derived from 'Tir Eoghain' meaning 'Land of Eoghan'.

Always remember one thing...

Beware of the monsters that may lurk under your bed, in the shadows or even in your head!